It depends.

ALSO BY WES HENRICKSEN

Nonfiction

In Fraud We Trust

Making Law Review

Poetry

Shouting Fire

It depends.

poems of law school life

WES HENRICKSEN

AYS
Books

At Your Service Books is an independent book publisher based in Miami, Florida.

FIRST EDITION

Dedicated to my students

CONTENTS

3L

It depends.

WHAT THIS BOOK IS ABOUT

Let me begin by explaining exactly what this little book is about,
That way you'll know before turning another page whether you're in or you're out.
In this book you will find 36 poems, all with a single objective:
To capture the essence of law school—at least how it looks from a student's perspective.

Each poem covers a topic of interest for students who seek a J.D.,
Straight from *Admission*, at the start of year one, to *The Oath* at the end of year three.
I offer my two cents on orientation, and outlining, case briefs, exams,
Appellate brief, law review, moot court and clinics, and a handful of law career plans.

But I cannot promise you'll find what you seek here, much less that I'll answer your questions;
At best, I will offer some thoughts and advice, with a sprinkle of tips and suggestions,
All of it written from my own perspective—not everything here's universal,
And some of it might be outdated, and some of it might even be controversial.

But I promise, throughout the book, I'll do my best to be totally open and truthful,
And, I should add here, a handful of my students have found a lot of this useful.
So, if you are ready, let's do this—we're taking this trip alongside one another,
Cruising through three years of law school and touching on one topic after the other.

1L

ADMISSION

The process of getting admitted to law school begins
with a fateful decision;
One that depends on the future you want, and the
kind of career you envision.
To be sure, it is a personal choice, one you live with
for better or worse.
It might be the best or the worst thing you do, so it
could be a blessing or curse.

Once that decision is made—that's the easy part—
then you will have to apply;
Find out exactly what each school requires, and do all
you can to comply.
You sit for the L-Sat, compose perfect essays, and
then fill out each application,
Making sure that you attach all your transcripts and
letters of recommendation.

Then you must pay to find out if they like you, or if
they will deem you unfit;
They force you to enter your bank account details
before you can click on "submit."
You cannot rest or relax until each application's
complete and submitted.
And in the end, after what seems like forever, you're
either denied or admitted.

But even if you do get in, you might well wonder if
you should actually go.
Is law school worth it? is something that almost all
1Ls-to-be want to know.
But this query misses a critical point—it's a strange
one, but I think it's true;
The question is not whether you should choose law
school, but if law school has chosen you.

Granted, it's just my opinion, or take, what we might
call my interpretation,
And I'll admit, I cannot prove it—it's purely a theory
of my own creation,
But the way that I see it, law school is a magnet; it
pulls people every year to it.
And once you're pulled in, law school's gotten a hold
of you, you have no choice but to do it.

It pulls people, not just from all walks of life, but
especially from all lines of work:
A nurse, a policeman, a middle school teacher, the
occasional grocery store clerk,
There's coffee baristas, and waiters, and cooks, not to
mention delivery drivers,
Tutors, receptionists, bartenders, coders, and all
kinds of service providers.

Wherever they're working or living, the magnetic
force finds them right where they're at.
Sometimes it finds folks while they're still in college,
and some it finds long before that.
The point is—it finds you... and once it does, well, it
will pull you in, sooner or later.
It does this by whispering into your ear: "*You are
destined to do something greater.*"

What this will mean varies person to person—we
each have our personal dream;
Some are quite modest and down to Earth, others are
ambitious to an extreme.
The catch is, though, no matter what the dream is,
you know you need a J.D. to do it.
And this means that you have no choice, it is out of
your hands, you have got to pursue it.

On hearing this message, most don't stand a chance;
they can't help it, they have to believe it.
Some start applying to law schools like crazy, about
as soon as they receive it.
Others fight back, they resist, or they try to; they
might hold it off for a moment.
But the magnetic force of the law cannot be beaten;
it's far too fierce an opponent.

The question is not what you want, then, but rather:
Have you heard that whispering voice?
If you have, then it's decided: you're going; you simply
have no other choice.
When you're being pulled by that magnetic force,
then—in my view—it's useless to fight it.
You might as well go to law school—in many ways,
you are already inside it.

You'll apply, and you'll get in—though, in truth,
there's no way you'll know what you're in for:
All of the dramas, dilemmas, and learning curve that
law school will have in store.
But, ready or not for what it will throw at you, you've
got no choice now but to do it.
That's what this book is for; that's what this is—if
you're up for it, then let's get to it.

ORIENTATION

Some days, you still want to pinch yourself; you can't
believe it—*you really got in.*
The first day of law school's approaching, you're
freaking out—you cannot wait to begin.
At the same time, you have questions, a lot of them;
there is so much you don't know.
At Orientation, you hope, they'll demystify how the
next three years will go.

Instead, what you find, as soon as you arrive, is a large
group of folks just like you,
Each without even the slightest idea what you're all
about to go through.
But Orientation is not just one day, no, they spread it
across the whole week;
With panels and workshops that, rather than clarify,
multiply law school's mystique.

A very brief welcome, then onto a session on
mindfulness and meditation.
You'll *need* these so you won't go crazy, they tell you,
for law school is not a vacation.
They go down the list of the mental health resources,
all of them totally free,
Which, they assure you, "Statistically speaking, at
least half you 1Ls will need."

The stresses of law school, they tell you, can lead to
depression, addiction, or both.
So, they add, you must take care of yourself, if you
plan to one day take the oath.
All of this talk of anxiety… *gives* you anxiety, right
there in your seat;
Your heart thumps, your head spins, your armpits
perspire, your hands and your face overheat.

You quickly make use of the mindfulness session; you
close your eyes and clear your mind.
When you open them up, you see they are discussing
the reading that you've been assigned:
"Getting to Maybe" and "Bridging the Gap" and some
other books on law school life,
And even some resources for your Support Team—
your loved ones, your husband, your wife.

A Contracts professor steps up, and she talks about
what to expect in her class:
The readings, the lectures, the Socratic Method, the
fact that some students won't pass.
The workload, you see, can't be carried by all, and a
few buckle under the weight.
This makes you hope, as you sit there in silence, that
this will not be your own fate.

The folks in charge then split you all into groups, into
this or to *that* breakout session;
They go over how to prep case briefs and outlines,
and then assign you to your section.
You learn very quickly that your 1L section will
separate you from the masses,
Dictating with whom you'll study and socialize, who
you will see in your classes.

And just when you start to feel comfortable, they
point at you—it is your turn to speak.
You smile and stand up, and you awkwardly wave,
your knees feeling wobbly and weak.
"Speak up," they shout at you. "Tell us your college,
your hometown, your first and last name,
And finally," they add. "Tell us—what are your plans,
your career goals, your ultimate aim?"

You open your mouth, and you hear words come out,
but it's tough to guess just what they were.
You sit down and try to blend in—but to disappear is
what you'd really prefer.
It's not that you're shy—okay, maybe a little—but
mostly, you're just feeling tense.
What you've learned so far has not calmed you down;
it has only increased the suspense.

At the end of that first day, you feel kind of like you've
been run over by a bus—twice.
Your head's overflowing with so many details, and
warnings, and tips, and advice.
But at least you're all done, so you plan to go home
now and crash-land on top of your bed,
Until you learn your section's going for drinks, and
so… you go and join them instead.

The rest of the week rushes by—a tornado—it's
spinning, and violent, and quick.
But one thing you *are* learning is the new language;
by day four, it's starting to click:
Appellant, appellee, petitioner, respondent—and
upheld, affirmed, and reversed.
Like any new language, there's one way to learn it:
you must become fully immersed.

IRAC and CREAC, and case briefs and outlines, the
holding, concurrence, dissent;
How "K" stands for contract and "P" stands for
plaintiff, how *mens rea* just means intent.
A tort, you now know, is a civil claim, where one
who's injured demands compensation.
And "Biz Orgs" is what everyone calls the class where
they teach you about corporations.

At one point, they go through the first-year
curriculum—Property, Contracts, and Torts,
And Con Law, of course, which will cover the
President, Congress, and federal courts.
But that is not all; there is Civil Procedure, and also
Crim Law and Crim Pro,
And in Legal Research and Writing, they'll teach you
the rest of what you need to know.

What's there to say as the week's wrapping up—
Orientation is almost complete.
Has it helped? Sure, it has. But it is not something
that you would want to repeat.
You've met lots of people who, like you, are
hardworking, idealistic, and driven;
Some will be allies, and others your enemies—but
isn't that always a given?

In four days, these strangers have all become family—
they're with you, for better or worse.
Folks with a whole host of interests and backgrounds;
the cohort's insanely diverse.
From zealous progressives who want nothing more
than to stamp out all forms of oppression,
To those First Amendment folks, hellbent on fighting
for freedom of thought and expression.

And then there are those who will focus on forests,
and oceans, and rivers, and lakes;
To save the environment, these future lawyers will do
it, whatever it takes.
From voting rights champions, family law folks, and
the passionate Crim Justice warriors,
To those drawn to taxes, securities, patents, and all
future corporate lawyers.

You're in the same boat with all of them, but they are
also all in it with you.
None of you, though, has a clue about just what it is
you're about to go through.
Whatever it is, though, you're in it to win it—to not
just survive but succeed.
With Orientation behind you, there's only one thing
left to do now… proceed.

MARBURY

But even with Orientation behind you, the whole thing does not yet seem real;
It's almost as if law school's only a dream; you can't help it, that's just how you feel.
As if it is—what? *Miles? Lightyears away?* Well, in any case, really far off...
Till one day you sit down and look up, and lock eyes with someone: your very first prof.

You look away quickly, but that's not enough, so you duck your head down, out of sight.
Calm down, you think, and you take a deep breath, but your head feels a little bit light.
And then, as you're slouched there, you suddenly realize you don't know what class you are in.
This sends you into a panic—in just a few seconds, the class will begin!

You rack your brain, wondering: *What the hell's wrong with me? Come on, you idiot, think!*
You wish to God that you could vanish from view, or at least, at a minimum, shrink.
Perhaps you could hide out there under the desk, just curl up in a ball on the floor.
On second thought, that would be foolish, when you could just get up and bolt for the door.

Instead, you sit up, look around, and you realize that
no one is staring at you.
You take a quick sip of your coffee, and that's when it
hits you—you know what to do.
You reach down and unzip your backpack, and take
out your laughably oversized book,
You slam it down onto the desk with a *bang*, and a few
classmates give you a look.

You stare at that book like you're hypnotized by it—
as if you're completely in awe;
Its title—two words—all in capital letters, declares:
CONSTITUTIONAL LAW.
Con Law! you think. How can *this* be class one? Why
not Crim Law, or Contracts, or Torts?
Hell, you would take Legal Research and Writing—
or any other 1L course.

Now, don't get me wrong, Con Law does have its
perks, like how it is always in the news,
And parts of it get people riled up based on beliefs and
political views.
The problem with Con Law is—how can I put it?—it
just...simply covers too much;
Where most subjects have three or four major topics,
in Con Law, you have a whole bunch.

What do I mean? Oh, you'll know soon enough, but I
might as well give you a taste,
To show you that your fear of Con Law is not only
proper, but very well-placed.
Torts, for example, has two questions: was someone
injured, and can they be paid?
And in LRW, they only want to know if you can write
and persuade.

Con Law makes subjects like these look pathetic, or—
rather—pathetically easy,
Just look at the long list of topics it covers, which
makes every law student queasy.
Let's start with the government—all of its branches,
and how each one interrelates:
Judicial, Executive, Legislative—and supremacy over
the states.

There's standing and ripeness and mootness, and all
other parts of judicial review,
And don't forget, there are political questions and
prudential requirements, too.
You must learn the powers of Congress, as well, such
as commerce, and taxing, and spending,
To know if a law they pass should be struck down, or
if it just might be worth defending.

Let's not forget all the personal rights, like the
freedoms of speech and the press;
How if you're accused of committing a crime, the state
cannot force you to confess;
The Establishment Clause says there's no state
religion; Free Exercise protects belief;
And if *you're* a gun owner, the Second Amendment is
where you will find your relief.

There's more to the Bill of Rights, but let's move on
to a whole other big Con Law section;
The one that includes birthright citizenship, and Due
Process and Equal Protection.
That's right, get ready to spend a whole week, if not
more, on the Fourteenth Amendment,
One context in which one might sue the federal
government as a defendant.

You sit there in class with that thick book before
you—you cannot remember the reading,
And the harder you try, the more distant the memory
seems to be quickly retreating.
Then, someone next to you says magic words; they
ask, "How about that *Marbury* case?"
Your brain goes from blank to filled up in an
instant—in fact, it is starting to race.

The case, you recall, is from 1803; it's about a judicial
commission;
President Adams had signed it, appointing Will
Marbury to the position.
But the very next day, a new president—Jefferson—
was duly sworn into office,
And the idea of his predecessor selecting the judge
made ol' Jefferson nauseous.

He learned from advisors the judge's commission had
somehow not yet been delivered;
And Jefferson figured this meant that the judge's
appointment had not yet been triggered.
And so, he said "No," with the stroke of his pen, and
he canceled Marbury's appointment.
To Marbury, who had been chosen by Adams, the
news was a big disappointment.

"I want to be judge!" was what Marbury said, and he
sued to obtain the position.
He argued that Jefferson had no right to stop a lawful
judicial commission.
Chief Justice Marshall, who wrote the opinion, said it
all comes down to three questions;
And thus, the Supreme Court's opinion got divvied up
into these three separate sections.

The first issue was whether Marbury had any right
to receive his commission.
Chief Justice Marshall said "Yes"—his appointment
meant he could take up the position.
Issue two was whether Marbury could sue to get
what he thought he had coming;
"Yes" was the answer; a right without remedy, after
all, would be worth nothing.

The third issue, though, was where Marbury lost—
and the issue was: "Can he sue *here*?"
The law at that time was not settled on this point, so
the answer was not at all clear.
Chief Justice Marshall stepped in, and his answer
would dictate how the law would go.
"*Can* he sue in the Supreme Court?" he asked. "Well,
the answer is simple—it's no!"

And with that, the would-be judge, Marbury, left the
Supreme Court that day empty-handed;
But far more important than that was the fact that the
Court's powers greatly expanded.
Up till then, it was not settled if courts could review
actions of other branches.
That case made clear that the answer is *yes*—one of
common law's greatest advances.

All of this comes to you—it's what you read last
night, and you wrote down in your notes;
You briefed the case thoroughly, started your outline,
and even included some quotes.
Your confidence rises; you pull the book toward you
and open it up to page one.
Now it's official, you think. *There's no turning back—
law school has finally begun.*

THE SOCRATIC METHOD

Some profs use seating charts, others use name cards,
  and others pull names off a list,
So many ways to choose who will be called on, and
  make sure that none will be missed.
This makes the first day of class unpredictable—sort
  of like playing roulette;
You will be hit with the Socratic Method, but don't
  know which version you'll get.

That day, your prof quickly shuffles some notecards,
  then pulls a card right off the top.
The chatter around you stops, everyone's silent; you
  really could hear a pin drop.
For just a split second, you want nothing more than
  to jump up and head for the doors,
But then the professor looks down at the card, and the
  name he reads off it… is yours.

Now—before you can panic, or scream, or pass out,
  and before you can even react,
Before you can think, *Why's he picking on me? Why am
  I the one being attacked?*
You sit like a statue there, frozen in time, half-
  convinced you misheard what he said;
You keep a straight face, you do not even blink, while
  a million thoughts rip through your head.

I must have imagined it, you think, *I'll bet every student here heard their own name.*
But then, the professor repeats it and, to your ears, it sounds exactly the same.
It sounds like the name that your parents have called you your whole life, since you were a baby;
And now you think, it really might be your name that he's calling—it could be, but maybe...

Maybe you're nervous and just hearing things, maybe all of this is in your head;
Maybe it's just a dream—you're fast asleep, safe and sound back at home in your bed.
Okay, probably not—but perhaps there are others in class with a similar name,
And it's one of them the professor called on—this and other thoughts flash through your brain.

But, you know how they say that the third time's a charm? Well, that day it was certainly true;
The professor reads out the name louder this time and, make no mistake, he called on you.
You stand up and wait to be seen, but the classroom has such a large size and enrollment;
The prof does not see you right off the bat—in fact, to find you, it takes him a moment.

A moment—a moment! What nonsense! A moment is here, and it's gone in a blink.
A moment does not give you time to reflect, or to worry or even to think.
But you do all three of these things as you stand there and wait, patiently, to be found;
You wonder why you came to law school, as you watch the prof up there looking around.

His eyes scan the room, panning left to right—and
then he stops, staring straight up at you;
He lobs you his first question: "Tell us," he calls out,
"just what is judicial review?"
Now, even though you read the whole assigned
chapter, and outlined, and briefed every case,
You don't have an answer, and so you just stand there,
an I-don't-know look on your face.

But then, you remember a quote from a case, and you
regurgitate it verbatim.
From the look on your prof's face, however, your
answer did not impress, much less persuade him.
He drops some advice—saying, when you're in law
school, and any prof asks you a question;
It's not to find out what you've memorized, but to find
out if you're paying attention.

And paying attention means several things, only one
of which is reading cases,
But that's just step one, the assigned readings—you
have to read and digest all the pages.
But on top of that, you must think for yourself, and
must come up with your own conclusions;
What the professors will most want from you will be
your own unique contributions.

You will be tested not only on what you know but
also, on what you think;
Merely repeating what this or that judge said, alone,
is a huge waste of ink.
Show what conclusions that *you've* come to, based
upon all of the facts and the rules.
The point is to not only memorize, but, in fact, build
analytical tools.

"So again," he said. "What is judicial review? And do not just quote something you read.
I'm *really* not looking for what your book's author, or this or that judge, might have said.
Think about all of the cases together, of how the whole doctrine evolved;
Describe it in simple terms, just tell me, straight-up now—what does the doctrine involve?"

"Judicial review," you say, "that's something courts can do based on Supreme Court decisions;
Courts can strike down acts of both other branches, at least under certain conditions."
"And what might those be?" he asks. "On that point," you say, "I don't think there's any confusion...
Courts can invalidate government acts if they violate the Constitution."

For the next several minutes, the prof asks you questions while disbursing key information;
That's when it hits you—the Socratic Method's an honest-to-God conversation.
The key, like in any discussion, is carefully listening to what is said,
And responding honestly, keeping in mind all the rules and the cases you've read.

The prof asks you questions, and yes, you must answer—but it's not about being "right."
It's far more important to be open-minded, quick-thinking, and always polite;
And also, to understand other perspectives, to view through a critical lens;
To always remember the right answer comes down to two simple words: "It depends."

The whole thing goes lightning quick—over in
seconds, it seemed, after it had begun;
The prof gives a nod, and he thanks you and moves
on—and that's when you realize you're done.
You simply can't fathom it's over, and that you
survived it, as you take your seat.
The prof then goes on to the next student—and your
Socratic discussion's complete.

It wasn't as bad as you thought it would be, but it
wasn't an easy thing either;
What you'd like now is to take a quick rest, or at least
get a ten-minute breather.
But no luck—your first day of law school's not over;
you've got one more class to get through;
And no matter how hard you expect it to be, oh,
believe me, you haven't a clue.

LRW

From Con Law, you head to your next class, which
happens to be Legal Research and Writing;
A class where we learn to write memos, you scoff, *what
could possibly be more exciting?*
The truth is that you are expecting a class that's both
boring and laughably easy;
Compared to the hurricane that was Con Law, you
think this will be sunny and breezy.

But this belief, it's like a dream that you're in, from
which you'll soon be rudely awakened,
Only to learn—your assumptions about LRW? Badly
mistaken.
This class, that you think so little of, is the one that
will affect you most deeply;
While all other courses will teach you material, this
class transforms you completely.

But it gets a bad rap because, its detractors say, "It
merely teaches you *skills*..."
And, to be sure, it most certainly does—that's the
primary aim it fulfills;
But as you are learning to write like a lawyer, you're
learning to think like one too;
Your brain gets rewired, and sharpened, improved,
and it shows up in all that you do.

And courses like Crim Law, and Contracts, and Civ
Pro—would all be quite useless without it.
Now, of course, they'll deny it; they'll say that I'm
lying; they'll claim I know nothing about it.
But what do they teach you, those doctrinal courses?
It's mostly just statutes and cases,
Making you memorize this or that rule, and a long list
of key legal phrases.

If that's what you gain from your law school
experience, I'm sorry; you're wasting your time.
Sucking up three years of your life to teach you rules
should be a federal crime.
And besides, all those rules, you could teach a
computer—a perfect job for some A.I.;
And if *that* was what law school was all about, then
we could probably kiss it goodbye.

For with the invasion of A.I., which threatens to
hijack the practice of law,
I've looked ahead at what's coming, or tried to, and
I'll tell you, here's what I saw:
Memorization is something machines can do far
better than our own brains;
And if we drop memory-based learning—then LRW's
all that remains.

It alone teaches those most-human arts, like analysis,
logic, persuasion;
How to distinguish, analogize, recognize truth, and
spot misinformation;
Not just to retain, but to closely evaluate what it is
you think you know;
And, on the ethics front, when to say "yes" to a client,
and when to say "no."

Critical thinking, in other words, you'll get from this
class, and this class alone;
And though no one says it, believe me, they think it;
it's something that's very well known.
Now, I am not saying those doctrinal classes are
worthless—no—very far from it;
But they are all down on the mountainside, while
LRW's up at the summit.

On that first day, though, you don't have a clue just
how crucial that "skills" class will be;
The influence that LRW has on your life takes a long
time to see;
You won't appreciate this class at first, but that's
natural, nobody does;
That's a big reason why it's not that popular now—
and why it never was.

One mistake that 1Ls make every year, which I hope
here to help you avoid,
And makes LRW faculty not just frustrated, but
super-annoyed,
Is the misguided idea that, somehow, this class offers
nothing they need;
They think that their writing is perfect, that they will
not have to work hard to succeed.

The most dangerous phrase in this class is as
follows— "I already know how to write."
Okay... maybe outside the context of law school, I'll
grant you, you very well might;
But no one arrives as a 1L having already mastered
this specialized craft.
Perhaps if their writing's exceptional, well then, they
might write a decent first draft.

But in LRW, you will discover, and have no choice
but to accept,
How clear you *write* reflects how clear you *think*—and
on both fronts, you're likely inept.
Most 1Ls hold strong opinions, but can't find the
words to back up or explain them;
They've spent their lives wielding words like blunt
instruments; honestly, though, who could blame
them?

Outside of law school, and even in college, or perhaps
especially there,
Careful attention to word choice and meaning are,
sadly, exceedingly rare.
So, naturally, when first-year students arrive, both
their writing and thinking are sloppy;
Lots of their sentences just do not work—they are
cluttered, chaotic, and choppy.

So, if you're like most, you will need to unlearn much
of what you were taught back in college;
Pages and pages of flowery prose will not help you
convey legal knowledge.
Precise, careful wording, and crystal-clear sentences,
that's what this class will require;
And *if* you work your way through five or six drafts,
then you might earn the grade you desire.

CASE BRIEF

In the middle of tackling the first assigned reading,
you're certain you're doing it wrong.
The cases are incomprehensible; many are also
excessively long.
You struggle for hours, and finally you realize— oh
God, it is not getting better;
Your head's spinning, and all the cases by that point
now seem to be running together.

There must be a better way—that's what you think.
And guess what? You are totally right.
There certainly is a way to simplify your assigned
readings every night.
If you paid attention in Orientation, they likely
explained to you how
To brief all your cases, but if not, then that's okay—
we can go over it now.

From all of the cases you read, all you'll need are: the
issue, the facts, and the holding,
As well as a rule statement, if there is any from that
case, which might be controlling.
These four things will be enough—there are others,
but these are what you really need;
They'll ensure you understand, and that you can
discuss, every case that you read.

So, now you decide to try briefing a case, and you start
with the first case in Torts.
The case is called *Van Camp*, and it is, thank goodness,
straightforward and mercifully short.
A three-year-old boy was out riding his trike when he
seemed to have gotten distracted.
A woman was walking in front of him, he did not see
her, and so, they impacted.

His trike hit her leg, and she fell to the ground; she
was injured and spoiling to sue.
She quickly filed suit against that little boy, and
against both of his parents too.
She claimed her injury was caused by the boy and
that, therefore, his parents should pay.
They disagreed, though, and moved to dismiss—in
plain language, they told her: "No way."

The problem, they argued, was that the complaint
that she filed was plainly deficient;
Alleging the trike struck her leg was a start, but alone
this was just not sufficient.
The reason is, in any kind of tort claim, whether
versus a child or adult,
The plaintiff's complaint must allege that the one who
caused injury is also "at fault."

If there is no fault, then there can't be a claim—was
the boy's parents' major contention.
This defense was not just well pleaded but, indeed,
caught the state judge's attention.
He granted the motion and dismissed the case, saying
with no fault, there is no claim;
It is unjust to seek damages from someone who does
not hold any blame.

You gather up all of this info, review it, and type out
your case brief in minutes.
It feels like you found a path through a dense forest,
avoiding the weeds and the thickets.
You've briefed your first case! You can't help but feel
proud, so you lean back and give it a look.
Then, you move on from *Van Camp*; now you're ready
to brief the next case in your book.

OUTLINE

Now that the semester is well underway, and it seems
to be going alright,
You spend every daylight hour deep in your
casebooks, as well as at least half the night.
And though you are keeping up—albeit barely—with
all of the readings assigned,
You have a sneaking suspicion, or fear, that you're
somehow still falling behind.

You highlight and underline, take lots of notes, and
you make sure to brief every case.
The problem—oh, just spit it out—it's your outlines!
Now, those are a total disgrace.
They're choppy, chaotic, disorganized—each time
you read them, you get more confused.
But why make an outline, then? What is the point, if
it's not something that you can use?

Here is the secret to outlining, which it is clear you
have not yet discovered;
It's not about writing copious notes about all the
material covered.
Instead, it is all about teaching yourself, and the
outline will be how you do it.
Once you adopt this correct frame of mind, you will
see that there is nothing to it.

Wait, you might think, the professor will teach me—
and isn't that, like, their whole job?
I pay their salary with my tuition, so if they don't
teach, I'm being robbed!
Well—I will answer—if you want a "C," then by all
means, sit back and be taught;
But I'm guessing you want an "A" or a "B"—am I
right? Okay. That's what I thought.

If you want a grade anywhere in that range, that is,
up near the top of the scale,
Whether your law school is Barry or Berkeley—or
Marquette, Gonzaga, or Yale,
You must take responsibility—for both your learning
and for your performance.
The impact that this frame of mind will have on your
grade is nothing less than enormous.

Teaching yourself, when in law school, means you
must create your own outline from scratch.
Using one that someone else made is always a
shortcut that comes with a catch.
The catch is, it's worthless. In fact, it is jam-packed
with unusable information;
An outline's true value is not what is written down
but, rather, in its creation.

The painstaking work of creating an outline is how
you will actually learn.
True knowledge is never given for free; it is
something that has to be earned.
So, how does one make a great outline? you wonder. *Is
there one way to do it right?*
*Where would I start, if I must make an outline—oh, let's
say—beginning tonight?*

There are a few things that seem to work for students,
pretty much across the board,
Which, I think, means out of all of these items, not
one of them should be ignored.
The first is to start early—do not wait until your final
exams are approaching.
Procrastination will kill your performance, regardless
of cramming or coaching.

Your outline should start on the first day of reading
and throughout the term it will grow.
And this brings us to the next piece of advice, which
is: always revise as you go.
Do not treat your outline like it's set in stone—it is
not; it is typed out in Word.
Leaving your outline untouched is extremely unwise;
it is also absurd.

Another tip: frame your whole outline around what is
in your book's table of contents;
From there, you can add all the rules and case
holdings, as well as your professor's comments.
Finally, ask: Do I understand all the material that I'm
putting in?
If you do, then you are doing it right; only then, can
you call it a win.

You're ready to outline, so you flip a coin—and it
turns out… it's Crim Pro you've chosen;
So, you grab that book, and your coffee—and then,
with a flick of your wrist, pop it open.
The book starts with searches and seizures, and it all
begins with a case that's called *Katz.*
You pick up your highlighter, take a deep breath, and
you get to work reading the facts.

BLUEBOOK

Every law student remembers the moment they realized the Bluebook's importance,
How that little book would weigh heavily on their own end-of-year 1L performance.
So, what is the Bluebook? And why does it matter? I'll tell you what you need to know:
The Bluebook is your only path to becoming a certified citation pro.

This matters in LRW, where you must dominate legal citations,
Crafting them perfectly is necessary to fulfill your prof's expectations.
And perfect citations are possible only by following all Bluebook rules;
This means the Bluebook will doubtless be one of your most indispensable tools.

How would I know? Well, I taught LRW for seven wonderful years;
And time and again, students told me the Bluebook is one of their ultimate fears.
Now… I disagree. It is not to be feared. But it is something to be respected.
Yes, it is nitpicky. Yes, it is dense. This is law school—those things are expected!

In LRW, I had a student once—let's say her name was Michelle.
She told me that, while in college, her teachers said she wrote unusually well.
But on her first memo assignment, her grade was a "D" when she'd wanted an "A."
So, Michelle went to my office hours to ask me why, in person, that very day.

Now—she was upset. And I understood why: she was under a misapprehension;
Her failure to grasp LRW concepts required a quick intervention.
Her writing had issues, sure, but when I looked at her memo, my main observation
Was the fact that, like most 1Ls, Michelle just could not write a legal citation.

The students who tend to succeed on citations are those—like in any endeavor—
Who put in the time and the effort, and through their hard work, they just keep getting better.
Their Bluebook?—They pick it up, open it, use it, and tab it from cover to cover,
With highlights and margin notes, marking the most crucial Bluebook rules that they discover.

Michelle got the message—I know she did because she turned her performance around.
The transformation that her writing went through was impressive, and even profound.
By the end of the fall term, her legal citations were flawless: a pure work of art.
To get to where she got, just open your Bluebook—it's never too early to start.

IRAC YOUR ESSAYS

As finals approach, you can't help getting nervous,
  and wondering what to expect.
Will all of the reading and outlining you have been
  doing have any effect?
What will the questions be like when you sit down
  and open your final exam?
What can you do in advance to prepare and make sure
  that you won't have to cram?

The answer is IRAC, a four-letter acronym that you
  pronounce like "Iraq."
Except that you put the stress on the first syllable,
  not on the one in the back.
Following IRAC ensures that, on essay exams, you
  will max out your score;
Whatever points you might have gotten without it,
  with IRAC you always get more.

The "I" in IRAC stands for "Issue," and this means
  you write down the question at hand.
It should be written so plainly and clearly, no reader
  could misunderstand.
To write it, you first have to spot it, to recognize
  issues involved in the question;
This is a vital first step—it's required; believe me, it's
  not a suggestion.

The "R" in IRAC stands for "Rule," which is always
the standard that courts will apply;
And so, it is crucial you quote it verbatim, or to at
least give it a try.
Sometimes the Rule requires more than one sentence,
and at times, a whole page or more;
You must explain what the Rule is, as well as how
courts have applied it before.

The "A" in IRAC is "Analysis"—where you explain
how you got your conclusion.
You should bring in all the facts and the law so that
there is not any confusion.
In short, you're applying the law to the facts, to decide
if the standard is met.
Practice enough essay questions, and you'll pull this
off without breaking a sweat.

The "C" in IRAC is "Conclusion"—and it's where you
answer the question presented;
Giving a clear "yes" or "no" answer is, ordinarily,
what's recommended.
Always keep all IRAC items in order—it's "I," then
it's "R," then it's "A,"
And last, is your "C," and your IRAC's complete; if
you've followed it, you'll be okay.

Is it really that simple? Of course not! But honestly,
what were you expecting here?
All you must know can't fit into this one poem, if I am
being sincere.
But now, at least, you do have some of the basics—
and I will give you a few more;
These are my thoughts—you can take them or leave
them—and please, feel free just to ignore.

If I were to ever do it again, here's how *I* would approach essay questions;
I'd start out by reading, with scrupulous care, all of my exam's written directions.
And with essay questions, I'd start out by reading the prompt that appears at the end;
This "call of the question" will set out the framework, on which my response will depend.

Next, I would read the fact pattern with care, while jotting down notes and my headings;
As I did this, I would not worry—yet—about typos, like grammar and spelling.
I'd spend fifteen minutes outlining my answer, and make sure all issues are spotted.
Later, while writing, I'd make sure my T's are crossed, and that my I's are all dotted.

Now I'm all set—with my outline complete, and with all of my headings in place,
There's only one thing left to do now—and that is to write at a furious pace.
Speed is key, as there is more to write than can be done in the time that's allowed.
It's crucial to flesh out each IRAC, to make sure your essay stands out from the crowd.

Throughout the whole process, I'd keep in mind essays are graded on organization;
Headings, and structure, and clarity—are given serious consideration.
The grader, you see, will read hundreds of essays, and so they must go through them quick.
Make your points obvious, cut to the chase, and don't try to be fancy or slick.

That's about it, I think, at least for now—at the
moment, that's all that I've got;
But even more crucial than any of this is to make sure
you practice a lot.
When it comes right down to it, I think the secret is
outworking all of your peers;
Doing this helps you achieve success, not just in law
school, but in your career.

CHOOSE THE BEST ANSWER

You've practiced your essays; your IRACs look great; and you want to sit back and rejoice.
But not so fast! Sure, you can IRAC an essay… but what about multiple-choice?
It's the flipside of the law exam coin, and you're sure to be tested on both;
So, multiple-choice questions are one more hurdle to jump over to take the oath.

Just like when you took the L-Sat, you'll once again face that familiar structure,
Which typically has the same three parts, regardless of which class or who's the instructor.
The first part's the hypo, or fact pattern, which sets out all of the facts you will need;
Below that—the call of the question—is often the first part of it you should read.

Then come the four answer choices—you choose one, and that's it, you win or you lose;
You pass or you fail, all depending on which of the four answer choices you choose.
Want to know how to succeed at it? Want to know my magic bullet advice?
Here is the phrase you should memorize; it's not just true but humanely concise:

You only get better with practice. Yes, that is it. There is no more to say!
To master the essay and multiple-choice questions, I know of no other way.
So… if you don't like the results you are getting, just sit your butt down and do more;
Only by outworking most of your classmates will you end up winning the war.

APPELLATE BRIEF

About halfway through your spring term, outside
there is an obvious change in the air;
It's warmer and sunnier, the leaves are returning—
but you do not notice, or care.
With the days getting longer, and winter retreating,
it's normally your favorite season;
But you cannot seem to get into it this year—you just
do not care, for some reason.

The fact is that something's distracting you, stressing
you, keeping you up every night;
And you and I know what that something is—you've
got a thirty-page paper to write;
A paper that seems to take over your life, from which
there's no escape, or relief;
With a name so ironic it's laughable—it's a cruel joke
to call that thing a *Brief!*

The Appellate Brief is an ordeal unlike any that you
have encountered before;
The memos you wrote were tough, don't get me
wrong, but this paper demands a lot more.
It's not only longer, and worth far more points, but
requires a new skill: persuasion;
And the mountains of research you must undertake
feels like writing a damn dissertation.

To top it off, it is prohibited for you to reach out for
any assistance;
And writing the Brief with no help will require
resolve and unwavering persistence.
But you've gotten this far, and so—well, you figure—
you'll finish this paper, no prob;
Just like with all other papers you've written, you
treat it like it is your job.

At first, you feel confident, pumped-up and ready—
it's scary, but also exciting;
You *dive* headfirst into the research, and think, in a
day or to, you will be writing.
But after a week reading hundreds of cases, your mind
is beginning to spin;
You can't figure out what's important, what's useless,
and self-doubt begins to creep in.

You feel like you're up on a mountain, halfway to the
top, and forgot how to climb;
This makes you doubt you belong there in law school,
and not for the first, or last, time.
But all of your classmates are on that same mountain;
like you, many think they can't take it;
They feel like they're falling, or drowning, or dying—
that there is no way they will make it.

For you and them both, when you feel overwhelmed,
just hit pause, and then take a step back;
Break the Appellate Brief down into pieces, which
one-by-one you can attack.
Start with the Cover Page—it, by itself, is
straightforward and uncomplicated;
You just need to know what to write on it, and where
each element should be located.

The Table of Contents and List of Authorities are
what you can move onto next,
But you won't be able to finish them properly till
you're done writing the text.
Then you can tackle the Statement of Jurisdiction,
and the Issues Presented;
It's not required to do it this way, but it's what I've
always recommended.

Then... Procedural History, the Statement of Facts,
and a simple Standard of Review;
And once you've completed these, you will have three
fewer parts of the Brief to get through.
And then, all that's left is the Argument, which will
take up at least half of the Brief.
As soon as you finish that, you will jump up—or
collapse—from pure joy and relief.

Okay, it's true, there are four more small sections: the
Summary and the Conclusion,
The Certificates of both Compliance and Service,
which can sometimes cause some confusion.
But that's it! You broke it up. Then just went
knocking down one section after the other.
And there's the Appellate Brief—done!—your new
baby, and you, the exhausted, proud mother.

Unlike with real babies, you should deliver the Brief
well before the due date;
So many things can go wrong, and it's not worth the
risk that you'll turn it in late.
You'll do it though, you'll complete it, accomplish it,
prove you're the cream of the crop;
Only through struggle and sacrifice, and of course
pain, will you climb to the top.

ORAL ARGUMENT

In 1L year they will scare you to death—at least,
that's how the old saying goes.
Who first came up with this axiom? I'm pretty sure
today nobody knows.
But the fact it's repeated by law students everywhere,
all the time, year after year,
Demonstrates that 1L students—yes, even today—
still have plenty to fear.

And the fear starts before classes even begin—with
the shock of those first assigned readings,
Then they're bombarded with Socratic questions in a
great many of their class meetings.
And throughout the year, their anxiety builds up—
both inside of and outside of class,
Knowing that midterms and finals await them, which
they hope to God they will pass.

Every night, reading and writing and stressing while
briefing a million cases,
Many will stop, and they'll think to themselves: *How
did I end up here, of all places?*
It's normal. It's natural. Or at least it's pervasive...
throughout the entire first year;
Many will wonder, as I myself did then, if law school
must be so severe.

But let's pause a moment, and take a step back, and
put all this in broader perspective;
Each student's view of what law school's about is, by
all accounts, wholly subjective.
And this sometimes causes the law students'
challenges to get blown out of proportion.
So, there is truth in the old axiom, but it also involves
some distortion.

The real world itself can be scary as hell—holding
down a job, paying the bills,
And just to survive, you will have to possess an
abundance of valuable skills.
Out *there*, there's no classroom, no safe space, no
mentors, no office of financial aid;
Proving yourself through hard work and tenacity's
the only way you will get paid.

So... *is* all this talk of how rough law school is just
some privileged kids having a tantrum?
The product of youth and a dearth of experience,
working together in tandem?
No, not at all! Law school really is tough, and the
scariest year is year one,
And all throughout much of it, students are miserable;
honestly, it is no fun.

And when it comes down to how scary it is, and
especially in that first year,
One event stands out from all others—for many
students, it's their greatest fear.
It comes at the end of the first year, and as it
approaches, the students freak out;
Everyone who has been through 1L year will know
just what I'm talking about.

No, not exams, nor the Appellate Brief—I am talking
about Oral Argument;
It is not just in its own category; it has its own whole
damned department;
It's radically different from other assignments or tests
that the students endure;
And it *makes* even cocky self-confident law students
panicky and insecure.

In OA, the students get dressed up for court—some
must purchase or borrow a suit—
Then they *go* to fake court, stand in front of fake
judges, and argue a made-up dispute.
The fake judges are not there judging the case, rather,
they're actually judging the student;
To see if the arguments they make are solid,
persuasive, well-stated, and prudent.

For ten minutes, the student stands at the podium,
trying to argue their case;
All while bombarded with questions from judges,
aimed to put them in their place.
The questions are jam-packed with technical terms
that the students don't yet comprehend;
Students, meanwhile, must just stand there and take
it, and wonder when it will all end.

Under that pressure, a few law students buckle, and
some of them actually crack;
I have lost count of the number of students I've seen
have a panic attack.
Some have thrown up or passed out, while a couple
have straight-up escaped from the building,
And one, this is true, ripped off half of their clothes at
the podium—I am not kidding.

Most students hold it together, though, they just get
nervous, break into a sweat;
Their heart quickens and their adrenaline spikes—
just the normal response to a threat.
For most, the whole thing rushes by in a blur, and
concludes unbelievably fast;
It starts and ends, leaving them standing there
thinking: *Have ten minutes already passed?*

They have, and they did—which means...
Congratulations on finishing your 1L year!
This is the first step, the base, the foundation toward
building your legal career.
With 1L now in the bag, you can relax, take a break—
why not take a vacation?
You have a lot to be proud of now one-third the way
through your law education.

What will you do during summer? Perhaps you can
work for a judge or a firm;
Or knock out some credits by taking a class or two
during the brief summer term.
Whatever you do, make the most of it—get some
experience, credits, or cash;
You'll see, that first summer, like Oral Arguments,
always goes by in a flash.

2L

RISING

That summer, they call you a "rising" 2L, but—
wait—what does that term really mean?
And where did it come from—from law students?
Faculty? Was it made up by the Dean?
My own theory is it refers to the rise in the number
of things on your plate.
If you don't believe me, you'll see soon enough—
being overworked will be your fate.

Your summer jobs, classes, and tryouts for moot
court, and tryouts for trial team too;
And then there's that whole competition for those
who are striving to make Law Review;
There's grades and class rank, cover letters and
résumés, TA and RA positions;
The angst of not having a clue if it's worth it—or if
you'll achieve your ambitions.

Many work multiple jobs in the summer—one for a
résumé line,
The other to live on, put food on your table, allow you
to pay rent on time.
On *top* of this, some are supporting a family, and
others have medical debt,
And others are dealing with as many problems as
anyone you've ever met.

So, yes, you are busy, and yes, your plate's full, but
still, it never seems quite enough;
You feel somehow no matter how much you're doing,
you're supposed to be doing more stuff.
All through that first summer, you work your butt off,
but feel like you're falling behind;
Without a clue that this is just the beginning, you're
just getting into the grind.

A classmate of mine back in law school, who I will call
"Bill," worked at three summer jobs;
At home, with his wife, Bill was hard at work trying
to win the relationship odds.
In law school, you see, it's inhuman how much of your
life those activities take up;
And because of this, law students in a relationship
struggle, and often break up.

Bill had been married for two years when he received
his law school acceptance letter.
He was excited, to say the least, and thought from
there, things would only get better.
But he and his wife got in arguments, honestly, all
throughout the 1L year;
Bill spent each night at the library; she kept on telling
him, "You're never here."

Bill had kept promising that, after finals, he knew he'd
have more time for her;
But summer arrived, and, well, wouldn't you know it,
it turns out that's not how things were.
In the morning, he clerked for a district judge, on the
fifth floor of the federal court;
In the afternoon, he interned at a law firm where he
offered them legal support.

In the evenings, he worked as a bartender-cook at a
tavern on Capitol Hill;
Of all the jobs he worked, this one was the only that
helped out with paying the bills.
His wife ate dinner alone every night, and she
pretended she didn't care;
But after a full year of it, she was tired; she hated that
Bill wasn't there.

Now, don't get me wrong, she supported his dreams;
on that point, there can be no confusion.
But in return, she got too little from him—and she
was, after all, only human.
And right at the end of that overworked summer,
Bill's wife finally filed for divorce;
And to this day, when he thinks back on how it all
went down, he is filled with remorse.

It's one thing, for sure, for a marriage to end, for a
man to let go of his wife,
For Bill, though, it was even sadder—he's certain that
he lost the love of his life.
But before you go feeling too bad for Bill, just think
about his ex-wife for a moment;
She'd had a life-partner, who, as a law student, quickly
became her opponent.

Stories like this one are way, way too common—in
law schools all over the nation;
Part of the hidden price some students pay just to get
a J.D. education.
In some ways, the first year's the hardest—and to be
sure, it is a brutal transition;
The workload, the midterms and final exams, and the
endless cutthroat competition.

But after the 1L year, do things get better? I must
admit here, they do not;
In some ways, the pressure might let up a bit, but the
workload gets worse by a lot.
But at least you have finished the first of three years,
and you only have two more to go;
You're still climbing up the steep face of the
mountain, and have not yet reached the plateau.

And so, though it's summer, you'll quickly find out it
is far from a summer "vacation."
It's just one more hurdle to jump over as you are
stumbling toward graduation.
Next year, the amount of work they pile onto you will
be profoundly surprising;
And it *won't* just be your obligations, but also your
blood pressure, that will be rising.

WRITING ON

There's a scramble for spots on the Law Review right
after finishing up 1L year;
It's almost as if students think it's required to have a
successful career.
The credential is seen as the ultimate accolade—
pretty much all students want it;
And in the end, they'll either love or hate Law
Review, depending if they are on it.

When I started law school, though, I didn't know
this—I'm serious—I hadn't a clue;
Up to that point, I can promise you, I'd never heard
of the phrase "Law Review."
I did not know any lawyers, had none in the family to
give me advice;
And more than just uninformed, I was naïve—if I'm
being completely precise.

But in the spring, Law Review editors hosted a short
informational meeting;
And told us all that, for a spot on the journal, we all
were already competing.
The grades from our first year, they told us, would be
given maximum consideration;
The top five of us, based on our 1L ranking, would
each receive an invitation.

But even if you're not top-five, they said, that does not
mean that you're all out of luck;
Every last one of you will have a shot,
notwithstanding how much your grades suck.
I found this last comment somewhat offensive, and
snobbish—but also, relieving;
Every time grades came out, mine were so bad, I
would spend a good week or two grieving.

They went on, explaining how after our finals, they'd
hold a Write-On Competition;
There at UW[1]—which was where I attended—it was
a long-running tradition;
The Write-On was open to everyone—all 1L
students, regardless of grades;
It lasted a week, but though it was short, it's a
remarkably tough seven days.

Here's how it worked at UW, which was similar to
how a lot of schools do it;
They hand out a thick packet—it took me several
hours to carefully review it.
The first task required is writing a short legal memo
that sets out a claim;
It should be polished to flawless perfection, or at least
that is the aim.

But that's not the only component; there's also the
Bluebook quiz, which will require
A scrupulous eye, and an editor's touch—your
citation skills must be on fire.
And then there's the personal statement, where you
are required to do self-promotion;
It covers diversity, passion, and work ethic—reasons
why you should be chosen.

The Law Review editors take all the submissions and
give them an overall score,
And then they extend invitations to those who end up
in the top three or four.
The rest of the spots are filled using a student's
submission score and GPA.
We asked what the formula was, but no matter how
hard we pushed, they wouldn't say.

I signed up to enter the Write-On—and when it
began, I jumped in with both feet;
Maybe it's my hockey background, but something
inside me just loves to compete.
I did it, submitted it, then spent the first half of
summer just nervously waiting;
After work, sometimes, to blow off steam, I'd hit the
ice for an hour of skating.

During the summer, the winners are chosen, and then
everyone's notified;
A few will find out they are in the club, while most
discover that they've been denied.
I got my answer in mid-June—they told me that...
hold on, wait, what does it matter?
In the scope of one's life and career, journal
membership is but one minuscule factor.

This is one part of the law school experience that's
always blown out of proportion;
Truth be told, missing the Law Review cutoff should
not be seen as a misfortune.
Like an "A" in a class, journal membership is an
accomplishment, but to be fair...
Very soon after you graduate, no one will notice it, let
alone care.

Yes, journal membership can be rewarding, but it has
its downsides as well;
If you join a journal—your family, friends, free time,
and life? You can bid them farewell.
It is a weight that's thrown onto your already
overworked, exhausted shoulders;
Like, as if you're carrying bricks, and they tell you:
You must also carry these boulders.

Now, some people think it's the damn Holy Grail, but
I promise you that it is not;
Just like the other prestige markers, this one gets
exaggerated—a lot.
Now, I am not saying don't do it; I'm just saying,
you'll be fine with or without it.
All you need is to believe in yourself, and you'll be
okay—no doubt about it.

PAYING FOR IT

Buying a house is life's biggest investment—for most,
this is certainly true;
If you go to law school, though, it likely won't be the
biggest investment for you.
Law school tuition is sky high, and it now costs
hundreds of thousands of dollars,
And law schools have now become factories, churning
out deeply-in-debt legal scholars.

This means that going to law school requires a well-
thought-out financial plan;
One more of life's lessons I never learned as a kid
growing up in Spokane.
But that does not make me unusual—*most* do not
know this; it's par for the course.
They smile as they sink into student debt, and only
later are hit with remorse.

This is why so many students—like Bill—take on
multiple jobs in the summer;
Not having money to pay the rent will transform
anyone into a gunner:
Someone who'll work two or three jobs at once, and
sleep only five hours a night;
Who jumps out of bed every morning frenetic to get
up, get out there, and fight.

For those who do not come from money, and therefore must finance their own education,
Which must include, I believe, the majority of the law school population,
Unpaid jobs like internships are so out of reach that it is not even funny.
For such folks, a summer job is not an option if it does not pay enough money.

This one little detail—financial security—weighs heavy on students like me;
As a rising 2L, it became all too clear just how tough it was going to be.
My loans piled high, and my paychecks were low, and I knew I would not soon recover;
Even with three jobs, I'm telling you—I only barely scraped by that first summer.

That's right, like Bill, I held three summer jobs—only one paid me more than a pittance;
When the fall term arrived, I looked back on that summer and happily told it: *Good riddance.*
But when I turned, and looked ahead at the 2L year, which was now coming my way,
I thought: *Oh, I see, they will work me to death, so it really is true what they say.*

In the background of all this are student loans, which I used to finance my education;
Something most students must do, if they don't come from money, in this generation.
Without taking on all these loans, many law students' dreams would not come to fruition;
No matter how hard you work, it will not pay your bills *and* also pay your tuition.

It's true, of course, what they say: you should not
purchase a thing that you cannot afford.
This is a piece of advice I agree with; it certainly can't
be ignored.
At the same time, I wonder: Was I in the wrong to
take loans out to get my J.D.?
To ignore the fact I could not pay the tuition, and
treat it as if it were free?

To go straight from college to law school, regardless
of what friends and family were saying?
To take out these massive loans that—even two
decades later—today, I'm still paying?
Was it all worth it? Did I make the right choice? And
should I have gone into debt?
Is it a choice that I'm proud of, or is it a thing I now
often regret?

If I'm being honest, I'd have to say here that my
answer depends on my mood;
Some days I think about all of my student debt, and I
am sure I got screwed;
But other days, even with my student debt, I feel
lucky to be an attorney;
Yes, it's been bumpy and painful—but that happens
in any worthwhile journey.

THE 2L SLUMP

Did they scare you in 1L? They did. But, of course, it
is not like they scared you "to death."
Now, they say: *This year, they'll kill you with work!* But
to you, they are wasting their breath.
After all, you did not just survive 1L; in fact, you've
become stronger for it.
So, what do you do with the warning they offer? You
shake your head, smile, and ignore it.

You smile through the summer and into the fall,
though you've never been more overworked,
Your constant grin hides the fact that you're
exhausted and often frustrated and irked;
You smile as you learn that your classes are harder,
the workload is far more demanding;
Last year your essays just had to be passable, this year
they must be outstanding.

You smile upon finding you must work two jobs,
while you're taking a full-load of classes;
You smile as your eyes cannot take all the reading,
and you're forced to purchase new glasses;
You smile when finding out your journal membership
sucks up ten hours a week;
You smile as you join one more student group, hoping
it helps land that job that you seek.

You grin as you accept an RA position with one of
your favorite professors;
What's one more topping thrown onto the already
heaping high pile of pressures?
You laugh as you're elected treasurer of yet another
law school student group;
And watch as your pile of pressures grows into a
towering mountain of goop.

You don't mind juggling, you've done it before—but
this... it feels like Cirque du Soleil;
You look at your list of commitments and think to
yourself: there is no freaking way.
And so, you decide: *It will hurt, but I have to take some
items off of my plate.*
You have no choice, in all honesty, you physically
cannot go on at that rate.

But one by one, you learn that each of these burdens
is there to stay—you can't back out;
Drop any one of them, and you are screwed, it will put
your whole future in doubt;
Lower your work hours, you will be broke—you
won't have enough money to eat;
Quit any extracurricular, and your CV will become
obsolete.

If you want to join a big firm or to clerk for a judge
or become a professor,
Or take any other path that might amount to a
prestigious legal endeavor,
It's not enough just to get the top grades, you must
also be overly active;
Being on Law Review, Moot Court, etcetera—is what
they find most attractive.

But all of it "counts"—therefore, all of it "stays"—you
just don't know quite how you will do it.
It's clear you are stuck, but it's not at all clear how the
hell you will ever get through it.
This is what happens, or some version of it, to a lot of
2Ls every fall;
They're overwhelmed and cannot see a way out,
which feels like they are hitting a wall.

Here's the solution—I know it sounds crazy—but try
to just shut it all out;
Close your books, turn off your phone, and log out
from your work and school email accounts.
Go for a walk, or just binge-watch a show; do
whatever it is you enjoy;
Take a day off from work, even if it means your boss
will be slightly annoyed.

Your mental wellness is far more important than
whatever's stressing you out.
This isn't news—it is just a reminder—you already
knew it, no doubt.
After you've given your body a break and you've
given your mind a good rest,
You will be not just recovered and ready; in fact, you
will be at your best.

RÉSUMÉS AND COVER LETTERS

You are not a piece of paper, but they tell you this is
what you must become.
You look for instructions or guidance, but still cannot
figure out how it is done;
How to flatten yourself, so that all of you fits on a
smooth, two-dimensional plane.
They tell you that this is what everyone does, but to
you, it's completely insane.

They call it a résumé, which is a concept that sounds
like it's simple enough;
To make a list of all your qualifications does not really
seem all that tough.
But when you attempt it, they tell you it's wrong, that
you've put everything out of order;
They insist that you make it look polished and
sleeker—and also: substantially shorter.

They give you a template, and tell you: "Now, make
sure you make yours exactly like this;
Even a slight deviation will make people think there
is something amiss.
You *have* to make sure that you blend in, and that
your page looks just like everyone else's;
If it has even a hint of uniqueness, it's tossed out, and
never progresses."

This is so stupid! you think to yourself. But you do
what they tell you to do;
You carefully comb through your résumé, and you
delete every last trace of you;
You take out the things that you value the most, and
leave in the stuff everyone has:
Your college, your major, your upcoming
internship—and all the rest of that jazz.

You hold it up next to the template—you're satisfied
you cannot tell them apart;
Your résumé's perfect now—no personality,
character, color, or heart.
The Career Service counselor gives the thumbs-up—
she insists you can call it a win.
Like all the best résumés she has seen, she says, yours
now completely blends in.

So, that's what you've now been reduced to—a black
and white one-sided singular page.
Everyone thinks this is normal, but you can't help
thinking it's utterly strange,
That in law school, to stand out, you're forced to
blend in, and to keep yourself totally hidden,
And letting out even the tiniest glimpse of your true
self is strictly forbidden.

But that's what you do, and you're done—now your
résumé follows the template's design.
Now, onto the next application component—which
they tell you is where you will shine;
A cover letter, you are told, is the place where you
reveal yourself to employers;
From district attorneys and judges to big city firms
full of corporate lawyers.

That's it! you think. It makes sense now. So, *this* is
where your qualities will stand out;
This is where you will convey who you are to
recruiters—you have not a doubt.
You sit down and write out what you believe to be a
sensational cover letter.
You revise and you edit—you polish it up until it
cannot get any better.

"What the hell's this?" the Career Service counselor
says when you show her your letter;
"This does not look anything like the template—I'm
quite sure that you can do better."
Template! you think. *Not another of those!* But you
decide not to say this out loud.
When she gives you the template, the message is
clear: Once again, just blend in with the crowd.

It has a list of instructions that detail what you must
put in every sentence,
With no room allowed for the slightest suggestion of
cleverness or independence.
You do as you're told and you write it again—and you
follow the rules to a T;
Making it, just like your résumé, as unoriginal as it
can be.

Now, the Career Service counselor tells you, you're
ready to go on the market;
With a résumé and cover letter like yours, you can
aim high, and still hit the target.
But she failed to mention that, when you're applying,
the thing you most need is: connections.
Because you don't know this, you're shocked by the
seemingly endless parade of rejections.

But don't let those bother you; if you're rejected a lot,
    you are doing it right.
When you enter the job market, you're stepping into
    the ring, so be ready to fight.
But it is not one-on-one, you are competing with
    many who want the position,
And so, you are always the underdog—vastly
    outnumbered by your opposition.

But it will work out in the end—you will get there!
    Just keep your chin up and stay strong.
If you're persistent and true to yourself, you will end
    up right where you belong.
How do I know? Because not long ago I was, more or
    less, right where you are;
And here's what I learned: if you follow your passion,
    then you cannot help but go far.

MOOT COURT

The appellate OA is now only a memory, but how
does that memory sit?
Was it as bad as I told you it would be—or did you
enjoy it a bit?
Was your main focus: *How can I survive?* Or was it
more like: *How can I win?*
After you finished the OA, did you find you wanted to
do it again?

If you came out of it thinking preparing appeals is
what you want to do,
Then sit down, let's talk about Moot Court, which I
think would be kind of perfect for you.
But not so fast—just like the Law Review, if you want
Moot Court, you have to try out;
For anyone wanting to join it, the Moot Court
auditions is your only route.

But let's say you join it—Okay, well, what sort of
experience can you expect?
And how about job prospects—will being on Moot
Court help or have any effect?
The first thing to know, and it's no surprise, is it will
suck up a ton of your time.
On the flipside, though, you get to travel as much as
you want without paying a dime.

You see, you'll compete at least once every term,
which could be in New York or L.A.
A few competitions are overseas, which means that
they're even further away.
But no matter how far you travel, your law school will
happily pick up the tab;
Flight, food, and hotel, as well as your drive to the
airport by Uber or cab.

But it is far more than a ticket for traveling—Moot
Court will change who you are,
Transforming you from an amateur into a total
appellate court star.
Bringing out skills that you've always had, but of
which you were not even aware,
And teaching you those all-important appellate arts:
how to best plan and prepare.

You must, of course, know the facts inside and out,
and the law you must master as well.
But how do you know if you've done what you need
to do? Here is one way you can tell:
Discussing the facts of the case should be like telling
someone what you did last week;
No one knows more than you do about this, and your
knowledge on it is unique.

If someone asks, "What happened next?" or perhaps
"What exactly did that person say?"
You know the answer because you were there, and
you saw it all happen that day.
That's how you must know the facts of the case; it
must be just as if you were there;
The key, then, is not just to memorize facts, but to
radically overprepare.

And then there's the law—like the facts, you must
know it like you know the back of your hand;
When it comes to applicable statutes and cases, you
have to have total command.
How's this accomplished? By practicing over, and
over, and over again;
Till answering questions from judges has become as
easy as counting to ten.

All of this comes down to practicing—endless mock
arguments based on your case;
If you will excuse the cliché, you must practice until
you are blue in the face.
That's how you win—you must go through more
practice rounds than any of your opponents.
This is the number one thing, although naturally,
there are a few other components.

Doing the research and writing the brief—these are
two more things that are required;
And helping out by mooting other teams is, not just
vital, but highly admired.
There's planning and fundraising, leadership roles,
and the budget for Moot Court engagements,
And coaching, recruiting, and helping in other ways,
like making travel arrangements.

If you are thinking that in 2L year, Moot Court's
something you might want to do,
In a lot of ways, it is like law school—you don't get
to choose it, but it chooses you.
Many on Moot Court have sworn to me, it is the best
part of law school—by far;
And one thing that's true for all students who join it:
they find out who they really are.

TRIAL TEAM

Some compare Moot Court to Trial Team, but the
analogy's clearly absurd;
You might as well liken a bottlenose dolphin to some
kind of tropical bird.
Sure, they're both animals, but to compare them is
pointless—it's also unfair;
One of the two creatures thrives in the water; the
other one, up in the air.

That is how Moot Court and Trial Team are—each
superior in its own field;
One's better if there's a case being tried, and the other,
if it's been appealed;
One's more prestigious, while many consider the
other more practically useful,
But neither one's really objectively "better," if I'm
being perfectly truthful.

What do the students on Trial Team do? To begin
with, they do a great deal;
Everything that must be done in a case before it can
go up for appeal,
From opening statements and witness exams, to *voir
dire*, which is jury selection,
And motions, discovery, closing—perhaps an
occasional hearsay objection.

Being on Trial Team educates students on how trials
actually go;
For those of you drawn to the courtroom, it covers a
lot of what you'll need to know.
The knowledge, the training, the skills and
experience to build up a solid foundation;
So… if they invite you to join, tell them "yes"—at
least, that is my recommendation.

TEACHING ASSISTANT

Yet one more reason to say "yes" is that when you look at your résumé now,
It's mostly just empty space, which you will need to fill up with credentials somehow.
But here's the hard truth: there are very few chances to add a new résumé line.
This means that you should be open to options—of every conceivable kind.

There's Law Review, Moot Court, and Trial Team—and these are great, of course, if you can get them;
But each one has only a handful of spots, and so most students can just forget them.
One option—too often overlooked—is get a job as a Teaching Assistant;
To get this position, you need not be brilliant—but often, you must be persistent.

Sometimes professors will hire a 2L or 3L to help with their courses;
By putting on workshops, or grading citations, or helping track down legal sources.
Sometimes the Teaching Assistants are also expected to hold office hours,
To help 1L students to learn the material and boost their exam-taking powers.

Some do the TA position "for pay," others do the
position "for credit."
Either way, though, it is worth it—and very few TAs,
if any, regret it.
It also will serve you by helping you build a
relationship with a professor;
Something I'd recommend law students do, if they're
able to, every semester.

So, yes, it will help with your résumé, but there are
even more benefits to it:
Professors will often write letters of recommendation
for students who do it.
And this can help big time in landing a job—giving
your application a nudge,
Whether you're aiming to work for a law firm, an
agency, business, or judge.

One thing I'd caution here... comes from some stories
that I have heard over the years;
Some TAs go on a power trip, thinking that they can
just brush off their peers.
They seem to believe it is perfectly kosher to trample
on their classmates' feelings,
By taking themselves far too seriously in their emails
and phone calls and meetings.

One TA, "Mike," went to work for a prof, for whom
he was to grade an assignment,
But it was soon clear that a sense of authority filled
Mike's heart up with excitement.
He changed in an instant, conducting himself as if he
was a faculty member;
He treated his classmates like they were below him;
it's something they'll always remember.

For example, he told students not to address him as
Mike, but to use his last name,
And anyone who did not heed his directions, he'd
happily publicly shame.
He emailed the whole class one night, and demanded
responses in under an hour.
He even gave some students "F" grades for simply
refusing to bow to his power.

No good professor—hell, no decent human—would
treat other people that way,
And only a certified asshole would even suspect such
behavior's okay.
Mike might just be one example, but through the
years, I have seen plenty of Mikes;
Those who get off wielding power, and in the end, no
one admires or likes.

Getting a bad reputation with your future colleagues
is very unwise.
So, if you have the privilege to be a TA, be respectful
to those you advise.
Do not be a Mike—be a mentor. Be helpful. Be
generous, and caring, and kind;
And if you can, try to impress the professor on all of
the tasks you're assigned.

RESEARCH ASSISTANT

Law firms and judges assess every applicant based on a black-and-white page;
That piece of paper is all that they have to learn what you've achieved at that stage.
So, any addition you make to your résumé increases employment potential,
And one of the most highly-sought-after ones is the Research Assistant credential.

It shows that you have worked one-on-one for a whole term with a faculty member,
And if someone calls that professor up, you'll be a student they'll fondly remember.
But none of this gives you so much as a hint about what RAs actually do;
Something that you need to know to decide if it's something that you should pursue.

An RA agrees to jump out of the real world and into a professor's mind;
And everything else, like your views and objective truth, must simply be left behind.
Instead, all that matters is how things *might be* as imagined by your own professor;
And your job is not to uncover the truth, but to work your ass off to impress her.

She—your professor—will assign you to research a
question that no one has asked;
To jump down a rabbit hole, chasing the answer's the
job with which you have been tasked.
But wait, I said *the* answer—no, that's not right—you
must locate the answer she *wants*;
To find the support for her pre-chosen answer—yes,
that's the required response.

Remember, the world you must navigate can't be seen
outside the professor's head;
A glimpse of its landscape, however, can be found in
what she has written and said.
The better you get to know all of its contours—its
shorelines, its rivers, its streams,
Will make clear to you the agenda she's pushing,
which helps you see what it all means.

Once it's clear what the professor believes, and you
see what she's trying to say,
Then you can log into Lexis or Westlaw, and get your
research underway.
Probing the depths of a question so narrow—it's tiny,
if not microscopic;
A classmate might well laugh out loud—and they
should—if you happen to mention the topic.

For instance, if somebody texts you an ugly emoji, can
that be assault?
Or what if you witness a fight, and you do not report
it, can you be at fault?
Does freedom of speech protect *whispering* fire? Or
what about insults? Or hate?
Can the Supreme Court be charged with a crime in a
lawsuit that's filed by a state?

Professors compete with each other to find the most random and unlikely questions,
They then take on RAs to help them, not only with research, but also suggestions,
On how to approach it, and how they might frame it, on which title you think sounds better,
Which of their theories appears to hold water, and which should be run through the shredder.

From the RA's perspective, though, is the job worth it? And what should a student expect?
Can the position be deeply fulfilling, or only a box to be checked?
The answer, of course, is that, like any job, it will largely depend on your boss;
Every position that you accept has its own benefits, and its own costs.

If *you* RA, how it will go will depend on the character of your professor;
And that, you will find out, for better or worse, as you work with them through the semester.
No matter who you might work for, it usually teaches you several lessons.
And makes you acutely aware of a faculty member's scholastic obsessions.

But if you are sitting there wondering if *you* should apply to become an RA,
And if you want my thoughts about it—if you were to ask me, then here's what I'd say:
I would say you should not listen to me, or to anyone—only yourself;
The advice you get should be tossed—not in the trash—but perhaps, rather, onto a shelf.

Somewhere that's out of sight, but still in reach if you
want it, or need it, someday;
Mostly, though, do your own thing—or as Fleetwood
Mac once put it: go your own way.
Blaze your own path, and reach for your own
dreams—listen closely to your inner voice;
Only by doing exactly that it tells you will you have
made the right choice.

CHEATING

People cheat all the time, and we all know it—in politics, business, and taxes.
Some people cheat on the ones that they love, and in school, many cheat in their classes.
In all of these cases, the cheater first works up a plan, and then works up the nerve,
To secretly steal something that they want badly, but know that they do not deserve.

Are cheaters bad people? No, don't be ridiculous. The impulse to cheat is quite normal.
Certainly no one is perfect, which must mean that no one is perfectly moral.
Cheating is something we all think of doing, though most of the time we don't do it;
We listen to our better angels, and in the end, wisely choose not to pursue it.

But... to think you would *never* cheat is an illusion—if you're alive, you're not a saint;
The drive to obtain what you do not deserve is both deeply ingrained and innate.
So, while we are tempted to look down on cheaters, and hold them in highest contempt,
We should remember the instinct to cheat is a trait to which none are exempt.

On the *list* of ways people cheat, law school exams
    should be placed on it, up near the top;
Every year, law student cheating is rampant; most
    likely, it won't ever stop.
The temptation is easy to understand—so much is
    riding on what grades you get;
A low GPA means your future's in doubt, but a high
    GPA means you're set.

So, it's natural to look at the top of the class rank, and
    hope that's where your name will be,
And this makes the scramble for top grades
    competitive to an outrageous degree.
The only way that one can move up in the ranking is
    killing it on the exam;
To many of us this feels, not just unfair, but, quite
    honestly, almost a scam.

I knew a student who thought this way—Irene—she
    resented the whole grading system;
When she got a bad grade, she felt she had not herself
    failed, but was merely a victim.
The whole system's rigged, as far as she could tell,
    custom-made to cheat students like her;
And deans and professors were basically tyrants—
    Irene believed that's what they were.

Well, any time someone thinks they're being cheated,
    it makes revenge seem only fair.
Just put yourself in the wife's shoes, if she learns her
    husband has had an affair.
The pain and the hurt seem to justify doing to them
    just what they did to you;
Screwing them over—that's what they deserve after
    all the shit they put you through.

And that was exactly how Irene felt—she was
convinced she was being "oppressed."
She told me she felt not the tiniest guilt when she
cheated her way through a test.
And nor did she seem even slightly ashamed when she
sat down and told me about it;
Apparently, she thought the ethical thing for them to
do would be to allow it.

Whether or not she was right doesn't matter—let's
put all the ethics aside.
Is it okay to cheat on an exam? That's for you and
your God to decide.
But here's what I've learned about cheating in law
school—I'll tell you here, just as a friend,
That even if you get away with it, it will come back to
bite you in the end.

And I am not talking here just philosophically—
karma and fate, and all that…
How the shame of it can't be escaped, and in fact, it
will find you wherever you're at;
No, what I am saying is, it doesn't work—it won't
even help your GPA;
I mean this with all of my heart—there is no chance
that cheating will get you an "A."

When it comes to essays, a well-written answer to
these questions cannot be faked;
What these require are mountains of practice—the
need for it can't be escaped.
With multiple-choice questions, it is the same story—
cheating won't get you ahead;
All it will do is waste valuable time, so, in fact, it will
hurt you instead.

And then there's the risk you'll get caught—which, if I may say so, is surprisingly high;
And if that occurs… well, just take your whole legal career, and then kiss it goodbye.
Students caught cheating get kicked out of law school, and won't be let into the Bar;
A process that's certain to mark you for life and will leave you a permanent scar.

So, how does Irene's story end? Let me tell you. To begin with, she never got caught.
But, nevertheless, after her 1L year, she was disappointed and distraught.
Her grades were so low, she got put on probation and was *this* close to getting kicked out.
She spent most of that 1L summer reflecting—her whole future now seemed in doubt.

That fall, Irene took a different approach—it was simple: she no longer cheated.
She outlined and studied and did practice questions—she put in the work that was needed.
Her grades, from then on, did not just go up—in fact, her GPA shot through the roof.
Today, I'm convinced cheating does not pay off—stories like hers provide solid proof.

IT DEPENDS

In law school, no matter what question they ask you,
the answer is always the same;
Yes, this is true; it's the very same answer—no matter
the topic or claim.
You could be studying Contracts or Copyright, Food
Law, or Health Law, or Torts;
It might even be LRW, or perhaps even Con Law or
Federal Courts.

No matter the class, when they ask you a question,
you give the exact same reply;
And if you stop and think about it, I think it becomes
pretty obvious why—
If a product arrives, and it's not the right color, does
that mean the contract was breached?
If a President claims an election was stolen, does that
mean they should be impeached?

Was a murder committed? Are the elements met?
When they spoke, were they under arrest?
And what about all of the evidence—if it is
challenged, should it be suppressed?
Did the one being sued meet the standard of care? Did
the state carry its heavy burden?
Should the court find that the plaintiff was negligent?
Are they a reasonable person?

To all of these questions, and infinite more, "It depends" is the only response;
Whatever the question might be, this is always the answer your professor wants.
And why—you might wonder—is this the one answer that they have all come to expect?
Well, it just so happens that it's the one answer that's accurate, true, and correct.

The world is complex, things are not cut and dry, there are myriad viewpoints and theories,
And somewhere in law school, you start to see there's at least two sides to almost all queries.
And so, if you're asked any "yes or no" question, it's never enough to choose one,
And then just sit back and relax, call it quits, and pretend that your job is now done.

This is what's meant when we say "It depends"—it depends on how you choose to see it;
No matter how certain you are of your answer, some disagree—I guarantee it.
On any conceivable question of law, you could argue for "Yes" or for "No."
And how well you advocate one or the other determines which way it will go.

And so, the true answer—the only true answer—if we're really paying attention,
If we are sincere, and attempting to get to the truth is our honest intention,
Then we have no choice but to answer with "maybe," "perhaps," or with some other hedge;
In most cases, "It depends" simply works better—and that is what gives it the edge.

THINK LIKE A LAWYER

When you got into law school, you probably thought
it would be an extension of college:
Some reading, some writing, a test here and there—
three more years of just soaking up knowledge.
But no! Law school is nothing like undergrad! Your
job here is not memorization.
From the first day of law school, you've been
undergoing a deep and profound transformation.

And now that you're just about done with 2L, you are
ready—it's time you found out:
The cases you've stayed up late reading and briefing,
they're not what law school is about.
The point is not somehow remembering all of the
black letter law, or the theory;
Instead, you are being rebuilt into someone who
knows how to think and speak clearly.

These skills emerge slowly but surely, through
lectures, assignments, discussions, and readings;
They're polished like stones in a stream through the
Socratic questioning during class meetings.
Little by little, this process transforms you—it's been
doing this since day one;
And while you're there, you will keep changing…
evolving… improving—until you are done.

It's *as* if you're in a cocoon for three years—when you
graduate, you will discover:
That you entered law school as one kind of person,
and then you emerged as another.
When you got to campus, your mind was unpolished,
your intellect underdeveloped;
It took you some time to get used to this new world
in which you found yourself enveloped.

Your thinking was clouded, your reasoning murky;
you were likely quite gullible too;
You probably bought into partisan dogmas you later
learned simply weren't true.
In '73, Kingsfield said it best—1Ls arrive with a
"skull full of mush,"
With a sense that you're smarter than you really are,
which professors will happily crush.

But as they do, you'll become sharper, and your
analytical skills will gear up;
The clouds blow away, and the murkiness lifts, and
your logic begins to clear up.
At some point, it happens: you *think like a lawyer*—but
what does this phrase really mean?
Is it a thing people actually notice? Or is it completely
unseen?

Oh, it is visible—very much so; folks will see it
whenever you speak;
The way you communicate, argue, and reason—your
method, your form, your technique.
You scrutinize words, and point out ambiguities—
you no longer go with your gut;
And arguments that they throw at you, you now find
are easy for you to rebut.

Your friends and your family will notice it first—
some will comment on how you have changed;
They'll tell you that you speak with much more
precision—that you're more alert and engaged.
But eventually, everyone sees it—the people you
speak with at any location:
At a coffee shop, hair salon, restaurant, or bar—
people notice in each conversation.

What will they notice? In short, they will see that you
know how to think and speak clearly.
This is a rare superpower—it sounds like a joke, but
I'm speaking sincerely.
The power to stop and to think—and to form and
articulate well-founded thoughts;
To cut through the cloud of political nonsense, and tie
your opponents in knots;

To scrutinize words with a microscope, so you will
recognize nuance and shade;
To understand better, more deeply, completely, the
message that's being conveyed;
This is true whether you're reading a case, or you're
watching the news on TV;
The ways many people manipulate language, you're
only now starting to see.

This power will open up many doors, but which you
choose will be all up to you.
And as you're approaching your 3L year, ask
yourself—What is it you want to do?
But whatever you do and wherever you go, and
whichever path your life might take,
Use this new power responsibly—please, I beg; do
this for everyone's sake.

3L

INSECURITIES

Have you ever strongly suspected that all those
around you know something you don't?
Like they'll all succeed at whatever they're doing, but
somehow you're certain you won't?
That you don't fit in, and you're scared they'll find
out, and that you'll be exposed as a phony?
That everything they say is perfect, and brilliant, but
all of your words are boloney?

This is what's often called "imposter syndrome"—in
law school, it's common and real.
Throughout the first year, and beyond, it is
something that just about all students feel.
Many predict it will disappear quickly—in a couple
weeks it will be gone,
But that is just not how it works for most students,
and so their prediction is wrong.

By the time I was finally a rising 3L, I expected my
fears to die down;
I was completely convinced that my self-doubt would
pack up its bags and leave town.
It didn't—as you've probably guessed at this point—
which is why I am writing about it;
In fact, for a long time, it hurt me and held me back,
simply because I allowed it.

What you should know, as you're set to begin the adventure of your final year,
Is that there's no reason to just assume your insecurities will disappear.
But don't get me wrong—it is not like things do not get better; believe me, they do.
It's just that the higher you climb up the mountain, the more that's expected of you.

A 1L does not even know what a tort is—at least, not until they are taught,
But by 3L year, every student's expected to know—and *does* know—quite a lot.
And as expectations go up, some fears fly away, just as some others arrive;
And meeting each one of them head-on is what you should do, if you want to survive.

So, don't expect all of your worries to vanish—they won't; they will only change form;
And perhaps, the best thing to do is accept *being uncomfortable* as the new norm.
If you are able to do this, and live this philosophy, you will go far;
So fake it until you eventually make it—or at least, until passing the bar.

BARRISTER'S BALL

Every spring, they hold the Barrister's Ball, and to go, you must purchase a ticket.
And as it approaches, you wonder if it's worth the price, or if you should just skip it.
Will it be a chance to have fun with your friends, and to schmooze with professors as well,
To stay up late dancing and drinking in the ballroom of some fancy downtown hotel?

Or will it be a drag—just a bunch of drunk idiots, all sticking to their own cliques;
Where folks who are not friends, or in the same social group, steadfastly refuse to mix?
Are the food and drinks free? Will there be entertainment? Is the D.J. they hired any good?
You call a few classmates to see if they're going—to help you decide if you should.

True, it is not the most crucial decision, but to go, it will cost time and money,
And to do it, you must give up Saturday night—which you could use to sleep or to study.
On top of that, there is a dress code, which means that you must wear a suit or a gown;
And then there's the prep time you spend on your face and hair, so you won't look like a clown.

But whether to go is a personal choice—which means, obviously, it depends.
Would you prefer to stay home watching movies, or a night out with some of your friends?
This is one question most law students ask themselves—in the spring term every year;
A low-stakes decision that—*hopefully*—has no effect on your life or career.

CLINICS

In most courses, you study court cases that are at
least one or two decades old;
You read them to answer just one simple question:
What did the majority hold?
You memorize rules and you outline throughout the
whole term, so you won't have to cram;
And when the semester concludes, you will suffer
through yet one more final exam.

A clinical course, though, is nothing like this—you
don't need a casebook or treatise;
There's *no* exams, nor any paper to write—so, you
won't need to think up a thesis.
A clinical course, instead, is something that is much
closer to actual practice;
To understand how, let's go over the clinical
education apparatus.

In a clinic, the law student handles a case that is
actually pending in court.
They work under a supervising attorney, to whom
they routinely report.
But the student, themself, is responsible for every
single aspect of the case,
From motions and hearings to meeting with clients—
online, by phone, or face to face.

Who the client is will depend on the type of the clinic
the student is in,
Most of which have certain prereqs a student must
check off before they begin.
Popular clinics include Immigration, Death Penalty,
Low Income Tax;
Bankruptcy, Juvenile Justice, and Health Rights,
among other clinical tracks.

In all of them, each case you'll work on is one which
is pending, and not yet decided;
Its outcome largely depends on the representation you
will have provided.
This means your personal efforts will actually decide
how the client's case lands.
So, *you* will see what it's like to have a person's case—
and thus, their life—in your hands.

In a clinic, you learn something new pretty much
every minute you work on a case;
The learning curve's steep as you soak up new
knowledge at a nearly unthinkable pace.
You hone legal skills while you're serving the
public—the key word here's "experiential."
And those who have gone through a clinic will tell
you: the experience, for them, was essential.

CAREERS

Law school is easy, compared to what comes next—
    and no, I do not mean the bar;
Oh, *we'll* get to that in a moment, I promise, but right
    now that's not where we are.
I'm talking about what you'll do with the rest of your
    life, what you'll do for a living;
In many ways, you're starting everything over, and
    your new life's only beginning.

This is a critical juncture, to say the least, it will
    determine your fate;
Each of the choices you make during law school will
    all carry infinite weight.
It's therefore a moment you'll look back on later,
    when you are much older and wiser,
And you'll either drop to your knees and give thanks,
    or you'll curse out your law school advisor.

Life is a tree full of possible futures—you start your
    life out at the bottom;
You're born in the roots, and from there your life
    moves up the tree trunk's thick vertical column;
At first, it moves straight and smooth, in one
    direction, it goes on this way a few years;
But then, at some point, it starts branching out into a
    thousand potential careers.

Each one, a path to what you might become, which
determines the career you will follow:
An eye surgeon down in Los Angeles, or an executive
up in Chicago.
Law school eliminates some of these branches—the
options you might entertain;
But even so, it's overwhelming, the number of
branches that still now remain.

Every experience, or choice you make, sends you
careening down one of the branches,
And from then on, it is down only that branch the
remainder of your life advances;
An email you send, or a web page you visit, a chance
meeting out in the hall;
A particular scene in a movie you watch, or a two-
minute telephone call.

Which makes a connection, or sparks an idea, and
suddenly, you are inspired;
And then you apply, then you go to an interview, then
you end up getting hired;
And then you work there for a number of years, and
that job becomes how people see you;
And if you don't like what you do a lot, you will regret
it—this, I guarantee you.

Once you have started down one branch, it's almost
impossible to ever go back;
Imagine you've hopped on a train, and it's barreling
at a high speed now down the track.
Do you *think* you can turn that whole train around just
because at some point you changed your mind?
Forget it! And that's how the tree works, as well—
that's exactly how it is designed.

So, choosing which branch to go down is important,
to say the least—hell, it's your life!
It's as important as whether to have kids, or choosing
your husband or wife.
You will be stuck with the choice you made, and must
live with it, for better or worse;
And every branch on that tree, if followed far enough,
ends up a blessing or curse.

Which it will be depends on just one thing, that is:
whether or not you enjoy it.
If you do, you should embrace it, but if you do not, for
your own sake, avoid it.
Too many law students start down a branch, and then
years later hate what they do;
This is a sad, but avoidable, fate—so, please, don't let
it happen to you.

The career choices open to law students vary,
depending on interests and skills;
And questions like: How much will they pay in rent?
And how much are their student loan bills?
Where do they see themselves ten years from now?
And how big of a house do they want?
Do they wish to live in a Manhattan high rise, or on
a lake up in Vermont?

Do they want to use what they've studied to go out
and work to protect people's rights?
Can they handle clocking up billable hours on
holidays, weekends, and nights?
Work for the government? Work for a firm? Or
perhaps go to corporate—in house;
And make sure you factor in how much time you want
to spend with your kids and/or spouse.

It all seems so complex, but really, it's not, if you look
at it in the right way.
Just focus on what you want *now*, and don't worry
about what might happen one day.
Work your ass off, and remind yourself that you're
intelligent, focused, and strong;
Listen to your inner voice, and do just what it says,
because it's never wrong.

JUDICIAL CLERK

In the scramble for post-graduation employment,
some jobs are better than others;
I'm sorry—it's true; it is one of those facts of life every
law student discovers.
Some jobs pay more, or they have more prestige, or
they're damn near impossible to get;
You know the jobs I mean—when you land one of
these, everyone knows you are set.

Other positions are less in demand, and do not require
stellar credentials.
Such jobs, of course, are much easier to land, but may
limit your future potential.
Then there are jobs at the bottom—the ones that pay
right around minimum wage;
And let's face it, lawyers who work at this level, most
clients would never engage.

Now, I am not saying that everyone goes for the same
top jobs, or that they should;
But this pecking order of post-grad employment is
widely-known, and understood.
Yes, some positions high up on the scale do not pay
that much money—it's true;
And some near the bottom might pay pretty well, and
could make for a good career too.

But we do not have to pretend there is no hierarchy,
for clearly there is;
And law students are not all equally qualified, despite
what anyone says.
Some of them outwork their classmates to such a
degree that it's not even fair;
And some have an I.Q. so off-the-charts high, that
their classmates do not have a prayer.

These students—those at the top of the class—all
compete for same few positions;
Jobs that will put them on track to eventually satisfy
all their ambitions;
The ones that, because they are highly-prestigious,
are naturally highly-desired;
To get them, the Law Review and perfect grades, are
not just a plus—they are required.

One of these high-status jobs is to work for a judge as
a judicial clerk.
The reasons are many for why this position is such a
beloved line of work.
On the practical side, it exposes you to an
unparalleled wide range of cases;
Running the entire gamut of matters the court's
jurisdiction embraces.

For many courts, this includes civil and criminal
matters of all shapes and sizes;
The judge hands these off to the clerk in their
chambers, which he or she then analyzes;
And handling such a diverse range of matters helps
sharpen your knowledge and skills;
From evidence, juries, and settlement offers, to
negligence, contracts, and wills.

Of course, there can be astronomical difference
between one clerkship and another;
Career clerk positions might last several decades,
while others last only a summer.
A "term" clerkship, though, is the standard; the term
that they last for is often one year.
They're highly competitive, and most who work at
them are early on in their career.

Clerk for a federal judge, and your future employers
will be most impressed;
And, generally speaking, the federal clerkships are
widely considered the best.
They cover all federal issues, from the First
Amendment to federal crimes;
And 12(b)(6) motions to dismiss the case, you will
likely see numerous times.

Clerking in state court might be less prestigious, but
it can be very rewarding;
And with all the issues that come through state
courts, you can be certain it won't be boring.
You also will meet many judges and staff, which will
earn you esteem and respect;
And you'll also build a professional network, with
whom, for years, you will connect.

Within either system—both federal and state—
there's a hierarchy in the courts;
The trial court's lowest, appeals court's the middle,
and Supreme Court's the highest, of course.
And clerking for each court will follow this pattern; a
trial court clerkship is great;
But compare it with clerking for a court of appeals
judge, and it will not carry much weight.

The top clerkship, then, is the U.S. Supreme Court—
there's literally nothing above it;
When future employers find this credential on a
résumé—oh, how they love it.
It is the mark of a young lawyer who'll, in the future,
accomplish great things;
In *both* public and private sectors, these captains of
law will be pulling the strings.

In all cases, clerkships are highly sought after, in
large part, for where they can lead;
A stepping-stone young lawyers use to accomplish
the thing we all want—to succeed.
Are clerkships the only way to reach your goals?
Well, of course not. They're only one route.
And I've pretty much seen it all by this point, so I
know what I'm talking about.

PRIVATE PRACTICE

Perhaps the most common career branch to follow is
simply to go into practice;
This will provide you financial security, as well as a
fair bit of status.
But how much of either it gives you depends on the
law firm's location and size;
Its office, its fees, and its roster of clients, as well as
political ties.

But no matter what kind of law firm you work at, it's
all about billable hours;
These are the bane of existence for lawyers, but also
what gives them their powers.
This is how lawyers get paid, you see, billing their
work time in six-minute blocks;
Which they track these days using not only ledgers,
but iPhones and digital clocks.

Practicing law is a stressful existence—your client's
life is in your hands;
This means that you must absorb their frustrations,
and put up with all their demands.
And throughout it all—above everything else—it is
critical to earn their trust;
Because...you lose that, you'll lose everything—your
reputation will crumble to dust.

The four categories of law firms are: White Shoe, and
Big Law, and Medium, and Small;
Imperfect though they are, these classifications pretty
much capture them all.
The first category is so elite, they'll take offense here
to even be listed;
If they had their way, people wouldn't have any idea
these law firms existed.

These White Shoe firms are so old, they were founded
when fancy shoes used to be white;
And they work with clients so big and important, they
try hard to stay out of sight.
Billionaires, hedge funds, and big corporations—
tobacco and opioid dealers;
They kill competition, exploit the tax loopholes, and
buy off political leaders.

The work that they do is so wrong, and so dirty, that
most people wouldn't believe it;
Whatever the rich and the powerful need, well, these
lawyers will somehow achieve it.
But don't judge too harshly—what they do is legal;
and after all, we're a free country;
And let's face it, most would do all that they do—and
much worse, too—for that kind of money.

The next kind of firm is called Big Law, and these are
the largest and wealthiest firms;
What sets them apart is not only their size, but the
income that each partner earns.
The list of their office locations is not just impressive,
but awfully long:
New York and London, and Sydney and Tokyo—
Delhi, Shanghai, and Hong Kong.

At firms like these, you will bill 3,000 hours, or close
to it, year after year;
You'll make lots of money, but live at the office—a
high-flying, hardcore career.
Though you'll have no time to enjoy it, you could buy
yourself a penthouse, or a palace.
It's a bit less prestige than a White Shoe position, but
nonetheless, very high status.

Below this, you have all the much smaller law firms,
of a more or less medium size;
Working for these firms is also respectable, at least in
most people's eyes.
The hours are not quite as high as Big Law, but the
income is not as high either;
Unlike Big Law, though, in a medium firm, you
occasionally can take a breather.

Then there are small firms, with just a few lawyers—
at these, you don't *just* practice law;
Failing to help out in other ways, here, will quite
often be seen as a flaw.
Apart from your billable hours, you must look for
clients by making connections;
And handle a bunch of the admin work, like client
intake, upkeep, and collections.

Of course, if you don't want join any law firm, you
always can hang your own shingle;
Just know that, if you do, your job is marketing, and
so, get ready to mingle.
The clients won't come to you unless they know you,
and so you must go out and meet them;
Work like hell, build their trust, give them results—
and remember, don't ever mistreat them.

There is so much more to say on this—I'm sorry, but
I can't go on here forever.
One last thing, though, that I'll mention is practicing
law is a sacred endeavor;
Our whole society can't be sustained without ethical
representation;
And so, you see, lawyers and judges are always the
bedrock of any great nation.

IDEALISTS

Then there are those who aren't aiming for money;
    they're working toward some greater purpose;
Their ultimate aim isn't joining a firm, but to work
    instead in "public service."
They want their job to mean more than a paycheck, to
    feel like they're doing some good;
They're passionate, driven, and idealistic, and often,
    they're misunderstood.

Some of these folks go on marches, while yelling out
    slogans and carrying signs;
Repeatedly chanting political buzzwords in carefully
    memorized lines.
Others might join campus advocate groups, which
    will stand up for this or that cause;
And some bring in speakers aligned with their
    message, eliciting boos and applause.

What sets these idealists apart from the rest is their
    certainty that they are right;
And so, if you contradict what they believe, they are
    ready to argue and fight.
But those who agree with them—they believe—are
    always virtuous, guiltless, and noble;
They're convinced they know the capital-T truth—
    and this is what makes them so vocal.

But the certainty many of these students feel is quite
certain to dwindle with age;
This will reduce how combative they are, and it
lowers their passion and rage.
Later in life, many doubt their beliefs—and they
question the causes they fought;
They second-guess many precepts and dogmas that,
back in their youth, they were taught.

Many young liberals move toward the center—and
some end up on the far right;
And some young right-wingers move so far left, they
start to think "socialism's alright."
But all of that happens much later, when life lessons
teach you what law school did not;
For a great many law students, fervent idealism really
is all that they've got.

And there's nothing wrong with that—we need
idealists, and they are key to our profession;
They fight for the poor, and for truth, and for
justice—they battle abuse and oppression;
They're our *public defenders* and *city attorneys,* the
ACLU free speech warriors;
The thousands of Justice Department attorneys, and
all kinds of government lawyers.

Some will be judges, eventually, and others, no doubt,
will become politicians;
Not long from now, they will occupy numerous high
level public positions;
They are the ones who will change the world, or at
least those who will most likely shape it;
Take a good look at those students, because they're
the future—you cannot escape it.

Folks my age see protests on their TV, and they
wonder: *What's wrong with those students—*
*They scream and throw tantrums, but don't know the first
thing of history or jurisprudence!*
But when we go judging those radical students, we
forget an embarrassing truth;
That they are *precisely* who we used to be, not that
long ago, back in our youth.

ALL OTHER OPTIONS

At this point now, we have talked about judicial
clerkships and law firm positions;
And all those career tracks designed to fulfill public-
service-related ambitions;
But that is not all there is—not even close! In the tree,
there are infinite branches;
The key is to look at what you want, and find the
career track that most closely matches.

There are *so* many others to choose from—to start
with, you could just go hang your own shingle;
A solo practitioner works for themself, thus
remaining professionally single.
Another choice is to go work for a company—this is
what's meant by "in house";
At my law school, down here in Florida, some
students go on to work for the Mouse.

There's also the Army, Marine Corp, and Navy—you
join up, becoming a JAG;
This way, you not only work for the public, but also,
you fight for the flag.
And then there's the legal academy, though this
branch is so small, it's merely a twig;
So few become law professors, but for those who do,
it's a pretty sweet gig.

Now, we could go on here *ad infinitum*... about all the potential careers;
On the wide range of ways you might use your J.D. in your precious professional years;
But I'll stop here—except... I'll mention just one last job... one which I did for a living;
It's a career that's as overlooked as it is underpaid and unforgiving.

It is the job of discovery counsel—a species of file reviewer;
This job's so low on the totem pole, that it is underground, down in the sewer.
Its bad reputation is undeserved, but it is nonetheless widely accepted;
If I had my way, though, this job would be better paid, and much more highly respected.

During discovery, which, in most lawsuits, occurs in its earliest stages,
Doc requests sometimes result in production of millions and millions of pages.
Discovery counsel attorneys are brought in to scrutinize each of the docs;
To go through them, one by one, until they've seen all the pages in every last box.

And winning or losing the case can depend on the contents of one single page;
Which will be located, or will be missed, at the lawsuit's discovery stage.
This makes the job of reviewing those pages not only important—but vital;
So much so, it should be a point of pride if discovery counsel's your title.

When it *comes* to your work, only one question
matters, and that is: *Does your job fulfill you?*
If it does, then you are set, but if it does not, it will
eventually kill you.
So, forget the whole totem pole—focus your sights on
the calling that calls out to *you*;
As soon as you see the path it's pointing out, that's
the only one you should pursue.

UPPER-LEVEL PAPER

As if you did not have enough on your plate, what
with classes, and projects, and meetings;
Outlining, case briefs, and day after day, all those
crushingly-long assigned readings;
And essay and multiple-choice questions on constant
quizzes and final exams;
The pressure of knowing you'll graduate soon, but
not yet having any set plans.

But *there's* so much more, there are extracurriculars,
like RA and TA positions;
Law journals, moot court, and trial team, or giving
tours to help with Admissions;
How about the fact that, to get a J.D., you must give
up three years of your life;
And likely broke up with a boyfriend or girlfriend, a
partner, a husband or wife.

And all the while, doing all this, you must network,
and intern, and send applications;
And you have no break, no relief from the madness,
not even in summer "vacations."
The heft of the stress, and your full load of credits,
and the weight of your fast-growing debt;
Makes you feel about as overworked—and
overwhelmed—as a person can get.

But you now see a light at the end of the tunnel—a
few credits more, and you're done;
You expect no more surprises—you think you've seen
everything under the sun;
By now, you figure, they've pretty much thrown at
you all that they possibly can;
But that's when they throw something else at you,
and it quite royally screws up your plan.

They announce you must do one more tiny thing. *It's
a small detail*, they say, *nothing major*:
*Research and write, and submit, an original thirty-page
scholarly paper.*
The name of the paper sounds simple enough—they
say it's called a "comment" or "note."
They insist it is no big deal, all students do it, and that
you're all in the same boat.

While that might be true, you just cannot believe that,
at this point, they'd do this to you;
A scholarly paper has nothing to do with law practice,
at least in your view.
According to the Student Handbook, however, to
graduate, it is required;
The same thing is told to you by every faculty
member, to whom you inquired.

It's pointless and cruel, and a little sadistic—at least,
that is how you construe it;
But no matter what it is, it is required—you have no
choice; you have to go through it.
You find a professor to supervise it, and you promptly
come up with a topic;
An issue of law that's so narrow and specialized, it's
pretty much microscopic.

You bury yourself deep inside the library—for weeks, you will not see the sun;
You promise you will not emerge, not for one minute, until your paper is done.
Coffee and Red Bull, and big squares of chocolate—the fuel you need daily to write;
You type till your fingertips scream out in pain, every day, and late into the night.

And just like you've done throughout law school, you pray for a miracle, and then you get it;
It's one more obstacle you've conquered—it tried to stop you, but you wouldn't let it;
You stuck to your plan, and you put in the work—you exceeded your own expectations;
Your argument's laid out on every page, and is supported throughout by citations.

You look at your paper, and half of you thinks it's a work of art that you should publish;
The other half of you is half-convinced it is the worst thing you've written—it's rubbish.
But for better or worse, you've completed it—and, hey, what does not kill you makes you stronger;
And while you still likely have ninety-nine problems, that paper's not one any longer.

GRADUATION

You knew it would happen, but still can't believe it—
you've actually come to the end;
No more exams, no more papers to write, no more
classes to skip—or attend.
It feels so surreal when it hits you, that you have
completed your law education;
The only thing left to do now is to put on your robe
and attend Graduation.

Just thinking about that day makes you excited, but
also a little bit scared;
You've spent three years of your life working toward
it, but somehow still feel unprepared;
That's because it marks the end of a journey, and also,
it marks the beginning;
This and a hundred more catch-22 thoughts bombard
you, and set your mind spinning.

Graduation... it's both happy, and sad—it's the best
day, and also the worst;
It is the last day of learning the law, but in some ways,
it's only the first.
It marks the day you are losing your freedom, and
gaining it—getting released;
And you can't decide if it's the most important day, or
if it's one of the least.

People might disagree with one another on what that
day's really about;
But all agree it marks a huge turning point in your
life—on this, there is no doubt.
And that is why so many family and friends go to
witness you walk on that stage;
Showing you that they are there for you as you go
through this life-altering change.

And that's who the ritual's for, really—it's not for
you; it's for those in your life;
Your parents, your brothers and sisters, your
boyfriend or girlfriend, your husband or wife.
So… when you *put* on your cap and your tassels, as
well as your robe with its colorful hem;
Posing for pictures and walking the stage—this is not
all for you, it's for them.

You see, they put up with you, all throughout law
school—hell, they've really been through a lot;
And *if* they want to get involved, or to get something
out of it, this is their shot.
You, on the other hand, don't even need to show up
there to get your degree;
Whether or not you attend Graduation, you still will
receive your J.D.

So, keep in mind, all of the pomp and the
circumstance—it is not all about you;
It's for your fans, your support team, your loved
ones—so, by all means, give them their due.
Show up and enjoy it, and smile for the pictures; it's a
day they won't forget;
Your big day, passing the bar, will be coming soon—
don't go too crazy just yet.

THE BAR EXAM

"Why not get rid of the bar exam?" some people ask—
it's a really good question;
Half the time, I agree—tossing the whole thing out
seems like an awesome suggestion.
Then I remember, it's easy to tear something down—
but replacing it's hard;
And some days I throw up my hands because, well, in
a few states, I'm already barred.

So, let's put aside that debate—because even if we do
not want to admit it;
As much as we might hate the bar exam, that does not
change the fact we are stuck with it.
And since that's the case, we should chat for a minute
about the best way to get through it;
How to prepare and to take the exam, and to not go
insane while you do it.

Step one is making yourself aware that it exists—to
just know that it's there;
Familiarize yourself with the basic components—the
what, and the when, and the where;
How it is structured, and how long it takes, and the
subjects most frequently tested;
This helps you focus on which topics you'll want to
be the most highly invested.

Now, bar prep is something you can't do alone—you
will need someone holding your hand.
You might doubt me now, but once you have been
through it, I'm confident you'll understand.
So, next you'll need to choose a bar prep provider—
there's BarBri, and Themis, and Kaplan;
Whichever you choose will become—for the two
months of bar prep—your closest companion.

Once you've done that, you should clear out your
calendar during the whole bar prep season;
For your own sake, avoid scheduling anything during
it, for any reason.
That means no trips, and no weddings, no birthdays,
no parties or social engagements;
If anyone reaches out for your assistance, tell them to
make other arrangements.

You have one job for those two months, and everyone
else will just have to accept it;
Every day during that period is crucial—it's your
study time, so protect it.
Every day during it, you make a choice—you will do
what you must, or you won't;
This choice distinguishes students who do pass the
bar, from the students who don't.

This is a choice made on each day of bar prep,
beginning right there on day one;
Continuing daily—a "yes" or a "no"—all the way until
bar prep is done.
This is what too many law grads don't get, and what
they just cannot comprehend;
The key is what you do each day in those two months,
not just what you do at the end.

By the *time* the exam rolls around, in a lot of ways, the
die's already been cast;
It's predetermined which students have failed, and
which of them have already passed.
This is because there is only one path that can
possibly lead to success;
And it's the one paved with your blood, sweat, and
tears—with sacrifice, struggle, and stress.

This might be overkill, but I can't stress this
enough—and I want it in print:
To beat the bar, you have to treat it like it is a
marathon, not like a sprint.
It takes consistency—you must put in the work
needed, day in and day out;
Discipline, fortitude, mettle, and grit—those are what
the exam is about.

The test is indifferent to how smart you are, how
creative, or how much you know;
It is hard work, and not brains, that determines, for
each student, how it will go.
If you are thinking I'm painting a pretty grim picture
here, you are correct;
Bar prep is, frankly, two miserable months, and so
that is what you should expect.

But you can take breaks! And you must take them. If
you do not, you will drive yourself crazy;
Take a day off when you need it, and let yourself be
just a little bit lazy.
No one can study for twenty-four-seven, for two
months—so, don't even try;
From time to time, you need to unplug and hit reset,
so that your brain will not die.

For some students, this means you schedule a day off, so that you work six days a week;
Others just plow ahead, working nonstop, until they feel their brain start to leak;
This is when reading makes more knowledge fall out, than a student feels going in;
Their eyes go blurry, their head starts to pound, or they feel the room starting to spin...

This is called hitting the wall—when it happens, immediately stop what you're doing,
Close the bar prep book, or program, or video—whatever it was you were viewing.
And put it away—what I mean is, put all bar prep books somewhere out of your sight;
Forget that the bar exam even exists—and take off that whole day, or whole night.

Every time your brain gets crammed full, and clogged up, the best way to get it unblocked
Is stepping away from it—when you return, you just pick right back up where you stopped.
Of course... all that said, you must do what you can to keep up with the bar prep timetable;
That day-by-day task list they give you, which students should stick to, as best they are able.

The more you complete, the more ready you'll be—so, do all of the tasks that you can;
This will involve, not just following, but coming up with your very own plan.
Find a way to teach yourself, and make use of your own preferred study techniques.
As you can see, it's a busy two months—it's like cramming for eight solid weeks.

And don't waste your time on what others are doing,
or how anyone else prepares;
Stick to the methods that work best for you—keep
your focus on your own affairs.
But no matter who you are, what your approach is, I
do have one crucial suggestion:
Make sure you get through an ungodly number of
realistic bar practice questions.

By the *time* the exam arrives, you should be so used to
essay and multiple choice;
That when you're confronted with bar questions, you
do not stress out, but rather, rejoice.
At that point, answering hours of bar questions is just
your daily routine;
You're nothing less than an essay and multiple-choice
question solving machine.

A couple more things—when it's close to exam day,
make sure you check out the location;
Plan your logistics, your travel route, parking, and
have some backup transportation;
Where you'll eat lunch, how the weather will be—be
prepared for whatever arises;
You'll have enough to deal with on that day—you
most certainly don't want surprises.

Finally, make sure that your tech is in order—ensure
you've downloaded the files;
Open them, make sure they're in working order—
then do one or two practice trials;
The *day* before the exam, you should relax—so, I
recommend taking a break;
Some people cram up to right before the exam—*I*
think this is a mistake.

And that's it, I think—or all that we have time for—
I'm quite sure that you will do splendid;
Feel free to follow, or simply ignore, everything in here I've recommended.
If you put in both the time and the work, there is no reason to be concerned;
The score that you get, like on any exam, is precisely the one that you earned.

THE OATH

You raise your right hand while reciting the oath, and
it suddenly hits you... you're done;
You got your J.D., and you passed the bar—now,
you're a licensed attorney... you won.
This thought sends you reeling; your mind reaches
back to the things that for three years defined you;
And somewhere inside you, your heart breaks a little,
to realize it's now all behind you.

The campus, the café, the hallways and courtyard, the
days sitting out on the grass;
Your study spot deep in the library, all of the routes
you took walking to class;
The casebooks, the outlines, the quizzes and memos,
the late nights you stayed up to cram;
The nervousness you felt each time you went into a
midterm or final exam.

Gone are your classmates, for better or worse, who
you saw every day for three years;
They are now scattered all over the place, busy
starting up their own careers;
A few live or work not that far from you, so you might
run into them now and then;
A lot of them, though—let's be realistic here—you'll
most likely see never again.

You miss them already, and not just your classmates,
but a handful of faculty too;
True, it's not like you miss *all* your professors, but
certainly, you miss a few.
You even miss things like the look of the buildings,
the landscape, the pathways, the trees;
There's honestly so much you miss about law
school—to greater or lesser degrees:

The foolproof excuse that it gave you whenever you
wanted to cancel your plans;
The parties that popped up to celebrate finishing each
round of final exams;
How every day, your outfit was up to you—you could
dress up, or dress like a slob;
The reason for this was the thing you miss most about
law school—not having a job.

Of course, though there are lots of things you will
miss, there are also some things that you won't;
When you take the oath, though, it's all over—all that
you loved there, and all that you don't.
Your life takes a sharp turn, and you plough ahead on
an unknown, completely new track;
You don't know where it will lead to—but one thing's
for certain: there's no going back.

This brings us to—dare I say it?—the end. Yes, I
know… it is hard to believe.
It seems only yesterday that you arrived here, and
suddenly, it's time to leave.
It's *been*, what I think we can call an "adventure"—
we've been through a lot, you and I;
Was this book worth it? I hope so. In any case, at least
I gave it a try.

I hope you enjoyed it as much as I did, or at least
found the book worth the price.
And with that, I'll wrap it up and send you off with
one last piece of rhyming advice:
When you are sworn in, and you're finally given that
well-deserved title: attorney,
Reach out and thank those who loved and supported
you throughout your law student journey.

ENDNOTES

FROM THE POEM *WRITING ON*

---

[1] Abbreviation for the University of Washington. Pronounced: *you-dub*.

ACKNOWLEDGMENTS

My editor, Hallie Guidry, did an outstanding job. Her eye for grammar, word choice, punctuation, and meter greatly improved every poem in this book. Verity Casey created the wonderful book cover. Tess Theisen and Anthony Portulese read early drafts of some of the poems, and offered helpful suggestions. Thank you, to all.

ABOUT THE AUTHOR

Wes Henricksen is a legal scholar who teaches and writes about constitutional law. He is the author of *In Fraud We Trust* and *Making Law Review.* Prior to becoming a law professor, he practiced law for ten years in California and Florida. He lives with his wife and two children in Miami.

Made in the USA
Monee, IL
17 May 2026

50359095R00090